QUILTING SHORTCUTS

·∴· Maggie Malone ·∴·

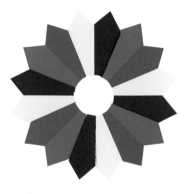

Photographs by Larry R. London

Ƨ **Sterling Publishing Co., Inc.   New York**
Blandford Press   Dorset, England

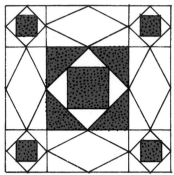

Storm at Sea, page 39

Sunshine and Shadows, page 53

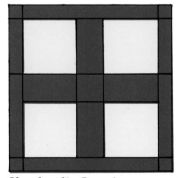

Shepherd's Crossing, page 49

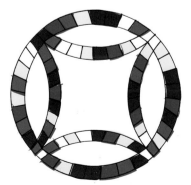

Double Wedding Ring, page 73

Edited by Barbara Busch

Library of Congress Cataloging-in-Publication Data

Malone, Maggie, 1942–
  Quilting shortcuts.

  Includes index.
  1. Quilting.   2. Machine quilting.   I. Title.
TT835.M355 1986   746.9'7   86-14440
ISBN 0-8069-4786-1
ISBN 0-8069-4788-8 (pbk.)

Copyright © 1986 by Sterling Publishing Co., Inc.
Two Park Avenue, New York, N.Y. 10016
Distributed in Canada by Oak Tree Press, Ltd.
% Canadian Manda Group, P.O. Box 920, Station U
Toronto, Ontario, Canada M8Z 5P9
Distributed in the United Kingdom by Blandford Press
Link House, West Street, Poole, Dorset BH15 ILL, England
Distributed in Australia by Capricorn Ltd.
P.O. Box 665, Lane Cove, NSW 2066
Manufactured in the United States of America
All rights reserved

CONTENTS

Nine-Patch, page 44

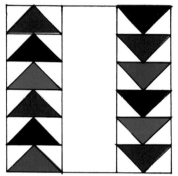

Flying Geese, page 46

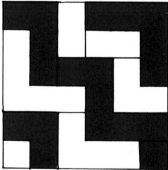

Endless Stair, page 41

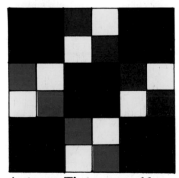

Autumn Tints, page 46

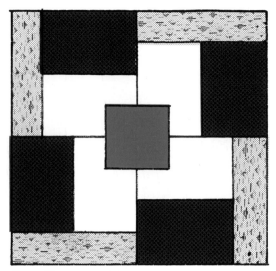

Swastika, page 48

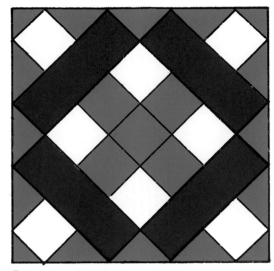

Casement Window, page 55

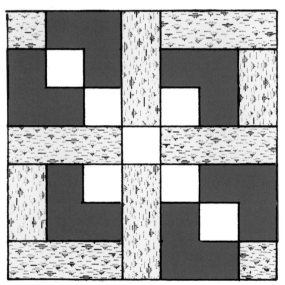

Leavenworth, page 48

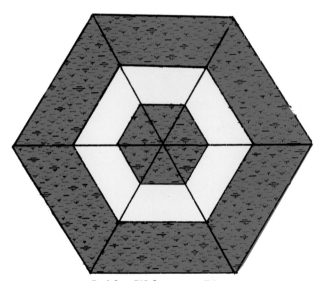

Spider Web, page 54

Pinwheel Squares, page 42

Mother's Dream, page 24

Cathedral Window, page 76

King's Crown, page 50

Lone Star, page 64

Mrs. Taft's Choice, page 96

Crossed Canoes, page 96

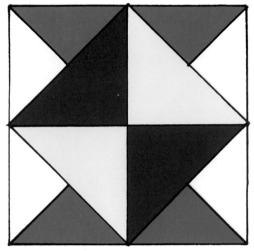

Southern Belle, page 95

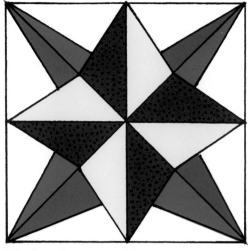

Blazing Star, page 68

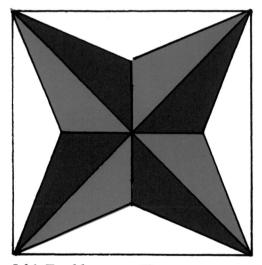

Job's Troubles, page 70

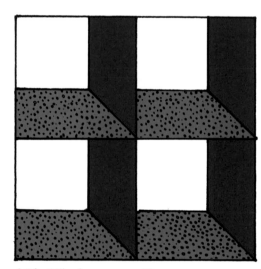

Attic Window, page 51

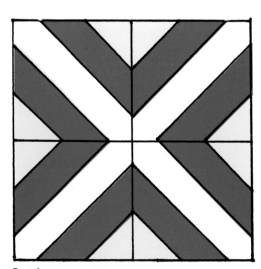

Lattice, page 52

Pinwheel, page 30

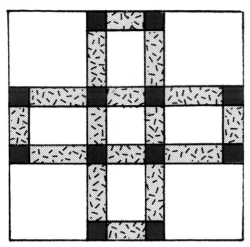

Tick Tack Toe, page 45

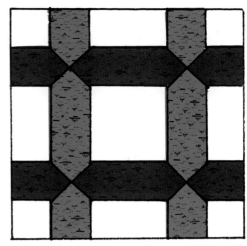

Four Crosses, page 47

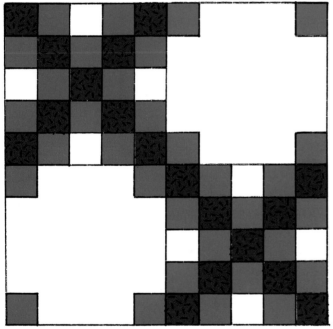

Double Irish Chain, page 44

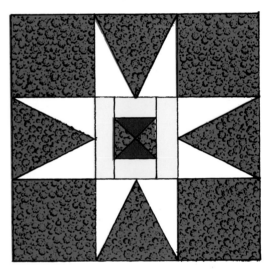

Dove at the Window, page 31

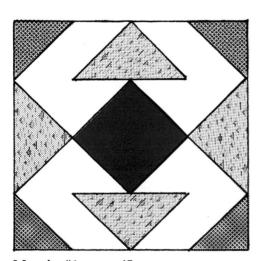

Mosaic #1, page 45

Rail Fence, page 43

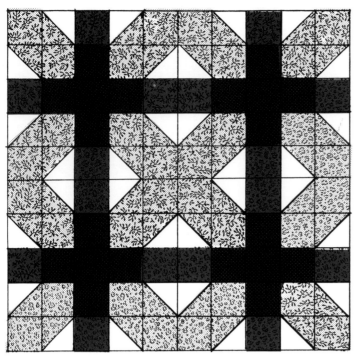

Antique Quilt, page 26

Spirit of St. Louis, page 43

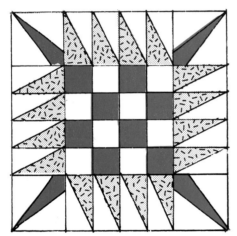

Thorny Thicket, page 39

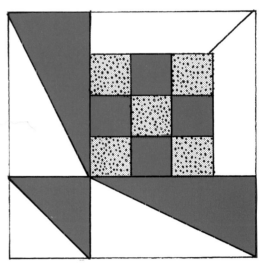

Bouquet and Fan, page 39

Basket Weave, page 42

Kaleidoscope, page 33

INTRODUCTION

I should tell you right off that I have a slight flaw in my character. I have a short attention span and like projects that can be completed quickly. I couldn't possibly entertain the notion of spending years on just one quilt. As I watch a quilt top take shape, I begin to see other patterns. *If I changed this part, and combined it with this block, how would it look? Maybe do it in yellows and browns. Oh, I know! Turn it on the diagonal, enlarge it for a medallion and add that border I saw the other day.*

Maybe it's not so much a short attention span as a vivid imagination. But I tell myself, *no, you have got to finish this top, you promised it to Mom for her birthday.*

Well, it wouldn't hurt if I just sketched it out, would it? It'll only take a few minutes. Umm, I like this, and I have the perfect fabric for it. It won't take very long to make up the center block.

Maybe Mom won't be too upset if I give her the quilt for Christmas.

Does any of this sound familiar? If so, this book is for you. The tips and tricks presented here will make quilting faster and easier than you ever dreamed possible.

Faster and easier does not mean inferior. In fact, I find that many of the strip-piecing methods, while making the piecing easier, are more accurate than if I pieced each individual unit separately. Corners fit squarely and curves match where they should.

Those of you who prefer the traditional methods will also find this book useful since basic patchwork, appliqué and quilting techniques are included. And many of the shortcut methods can be executed by hand as well as by machine. The appendix contains a number of popular patterns, all of which can be adapted to the shortcut methods. These patterns are not shown in the color index in the front.

Actually, I've tried to compile a book that covers the needs of most quilters. Want to try English piecing? It's in here. Want to know how to make a continuous bias binding or how to mitre corners? It's in here. In fact, I've tried to include just about everything I've learned in 20 years of quilt making.

I'm hoping that you will profit from my experience and will find this to be a truly indispensable addition to your quilt book collection.

TOOLS
OF THE TRADE

The tools needed for quilt making are relatively simple and if you have done any sewing you probably have most of them already. Once you're hooked, however, you may be interested in acquiring some of the nifty little gadgets that make the whole process faster or easier. Those marked with an asterisk are essential.

Cutting Tools

*Scissors. A really good, sharp pair of scissors is essential. Fiskars or Ginghers are both very good, cutting up to six or eight layers of fabric at one time.

Rotary Cutter. If you like strip-piecing, you'll find this tool indispensable for cutting long strips. You can stack your fabric in six to eight layers and using a straightedge, cut strips in no time at all. Once you've assembled the strips, stack them up again and cut several at once.

X-acto Knife. This is a handy tool for cutting out templates and quilting stencils.

Rulers and Templates

*Ruler. Any type of ruler can be used as long as it is perfectly straight and accurate. The plastic transparent rulers, in either 12" or 18" lengths are preferred by many quilters because the markings on the rulers allow you to make perfect squares and angles.

Precut Plastic Strips. These are available commercially in widths of 1" to 3½" and 24" long. You could make your own from Plexiglas (acrylic plastic), long enough to fit across the entire width of fabric, but you must be sure that they are absolutely accurate. A few small squares of sandpaper glued to one side will help prevent slippage. Use these strips to mark directly on the fabric and with your rotary cutter.

Ready-made Templates. Quilt shops carry a wide assortment of templates for many traditional patterns in both metal and plastic. The metal ones are of the cutout type allowing you to mark both the seam line and the cutting line. However, for some of the more unusual designs, you will have to make your own templates.

Cardboard, such as that of tablet backs or soap cartons, is the most common material used for templates. It is easy to come by and easy to cut. Its major drawback is that it wears down quickly; so you should make several templates to complete the marking of one quilt. Back them with sandpaper to prevent slipping on the fabric.

If you use sheets of plastic for your templates, you eliminate the wear problem. Most quilt shops now carry these sheets in packages of two. Again, back them with sandpaper to prevent slipping.

Check the packaging materials that you bring into your home for suitable plastic for templates. Coffee-can lids are of a good sturdy plastic for smaller pieces. Some meats are packaged in plastic trays, which can be easily cut into templates.

Marking Tools

*Pencils. For marking pieces for cutting, a soft, dark lead pencil or a fine-line ballpoint pen can be used. For seam lines, use a hard lead pencil since it won't smudge as easily. Be sure the pencil is sharp at all times.

Dressmaker's Pencils. These are nice to have on hand for marking dark fabrics.

For marking the quilting design on the top, your main consideration is that the marks be easily removed. A hard lead pencil won't smudge, leaving dirty marks on the top, and its markings will usually wash out in the first washing.

Dressmaker's pencils or tailor's chalk will usually brush off. For this reason, only small portions of the top should be marked at one time. Small slivers of soap are also good for drawing fairly straight lines.

Carpenter's Chalk. This is usually blue in color and, along with a line, can be used for straight-line designs across the quilt top. The chalk can also be used with perforated patterns.

Dressmaker's Carbon Paper. Use this with a tracing wheel for relatively simple designs. For more intricate patterns, switch to a ballpoint pen for marking through the carbon paper. *One caution:* If using the dark-blue carbon, it may take several washings to remove all traces of the markings.

Next to your needle or sewing machine, your iron is the most important tool for achieving outstanding results. I can't emphasize enough the necessity of ironing each seam to one side before joining it to a cross-seam, to ensure a smooth flat top.

Instead of jumping up and down to run to the ironing board, bring the iron to you. If you have an adjustable ironing board, set it at a convenient height and place it right by your chair. If it isn't adjustable, pull a small table close to your chair and cover it with a doubled bath towel. Plug in your iron and you're all set. I do a lot of sewing at the kitchen table; so I just lay the towel next to the machine. This way, I don't have any excuses for not ironing a seam.

FABRIC
SELECTION

The favorite fabric of quilters is 100 percent cotton. Its smooth, soft finish allows the needle to glide easily through the fabric during both the piecing and quilting processes.

Fabric availability is subject to fashion trends. Right now, natural fabrics are in good supply, but next year may be different and cotton hard to come by. Color and print selections may also be limited. Cotton is also subject to fading and shrinking.

The cotton/polyester blends are an excellent choice for quilting. They are always available, come in a wide range of colors and prints, do not fade or shrink, and are almost as easy as cotton to sew.

The big question in choosing cotton blends over cotton is durability. The cotton blends haven't been around long enough to compare to a hundred-year-old cotton quilt, but in fairness, you should keep in mind that most of those antique quilts were not subjected to frequent washing in harsh chemicals. In fact, most of the examples that have survived to the present were "best quilts" that were taken out to

honor special guests, then either packed away or placed in a dark, unused bedroom.

If you are using a sewing machine, ease of sewing need not be a prime consideration in your choice of fabric. The piecing can be done on the machine, and the finished top can be tied or machine-quilted.

Wool is a lovely fabric, available in a wide range of colors and weights. The heavier wools would be excellent candidates for a tied quilt, while the lighter-weight wools can be machine-quilted, or even hand-quilted.

Denim and corduroy are fine choices for children's quilts. These fabrics can take all the abuse a child will give it and stand up well to the frequent washings necessary. They are also good choices for a masculine quilt, giving a rugged texture that many men like.

Many modern quilters have incorporated the polyester double knits into their quilts with good results. Some of these do have a tendency to pill or snag though, so a hard, smooth weave would be preferable to a nubby finish.

T-shirts have even made their way into quilting. With all the designs being printed on them, they make a really fun quilt top. Because of the stretch in T-shirt material, however, it is necessary to back the fabric with very light-weight iron-on interfacing.

Velvets, velveteens, silks and satins were used in old quilts, especially the crazy quilts. They are suitable for a very special quilt that won't see a lot of hard wear since the real thing is easily damaged and must be dry-cleaned. We do have the advantage of modern imitation velvets, silks and satins made from synthetics that give the appearance and texture of those luscious fabrics without the necessity of special care.

Scraps of new fabrics from other sewing projects can also be used to advantage by using many of the shortcut methods in this book. A word of warning should be given, however, about using worn clothing for quilt making. *Do not* use worn or threadbare sections of garments in your quilt, only those areas that are still strong and look almost new. Worn pieces of cloth will wear out much quicker than newer pieces so that your quilt will not last as long as it should. After all the hours you spend making your quilt, you don't want it to look worn and tired within a year or two.

The choice of backing material is almost as broad as that for the top. You can select one of the fabrics used in the top for the back. Approximately six yards of fabric are needed for a double-size bed.

A bed sheet is an excellent choice, available in a wide range of prints and pastels. The real beauty of using a sheet is that you can buy the sheet the right size to fit the quilt top with no piecing of strips for the back. Muslin (calico) is the best choice since it is easier to sew. It should be washed before use to remove all sizing.

My personal favorite for backing a quilt is flannel. Even though I have to piece the back, the soft cuddly warmth of it makes it well worthwhile. Flannel sheets are becoming readily available so you may not even have to seam the pieces together. Of course, you don't pay a lot for a flannel sheet just to back a quilt. Since they are a seasonal item, wait for the spring closeouts to stock up. I picked up several double-size sheets last spring at my local discount store for a few dollars each. I can't even buy flannel yard goods that cheaply.

Batts and Fillers

This is the material that goes between the top and the backing. In the past, every imaginable material has been used for this purpose, from corn husks to straw to raw cotton. Old blankets and worn quilts were often recycled as fillers for new quilts. Needless to say, such quilts were usually tied rather than quilted.

Until recent years, the cotton batt was the only one available. If you are trying to emulate the look of an antique quilt, this is the batt to use. It gives a flat appearance to the finished quilting. This batt must be closely quilted. There should be no more than an inch between lines of quilting or it will bunch up and shift when washed.

Bonded polyester batts are made of a polyester material, which has been treated with a glaze to hold the fibres together. It is easy to work with since the layers of the batt will not shred or tear, giving a smooth uniform surface. The finished quilt has a puffy look, and the quilting stitches stand out in sharp relief to the background. Since it will not shift, it can be quilted in lines up to 4 inches apart.

Unbonded batts are also of synthetic materials, but they have not been treated with the glazing chemicals. This gives a puffier look to the finished quilt than the bonded batts. Care must be taken in spreading the batt on the top because it will shred or tear, causing thick and thin spots. This is easily fixed by pulling fibres from the thick spots or from the edges to fill in the thin spots. Once quilted, the batt will not shift, so that quilting can be done in lines up to 4 inches apart.

QUILT SIZE

The starting point in determining the size of the finished quilt is the mattress size. This is especially important when making a medallion type of quilt or some of the appliqué designs. For this type of design you want the focal point of the quilt to be properly centered on the mattress with the borders falling from the sides.

As a general guideline, mattress sizes are as follows:

Crib	27″ × 50″
Single/Cot	30″ × 75″
Twin	39″ × 75″
Double	54″ × 75″
Queen	60″ × 80″
King	72″ × 84″

If your mattress is old and suffers from middle-age spread, you should measure it. There could be an inch or so difference in the size of yours and its standard size when new.

Now, do you want to tuck the quilt under the pillows? A general allowance is 18″, but there is so much difference in the size of pillows that you should probably measure to be sure. My husband has a fairly new foam-filled pillow, which rises twice as high as my 20-year-old feather pillow.

To measure, make up the bed with a bedspread that fits the way you like it. Take a tape measure and place it under the pillow as far back as the fold of the spread. Bring the tape up over the mattress and to the back of the pillows. Add this figure to the length of the quilt.

For the overhang at bottom and sides, measure the depth of the box springs and mattress. If you have a bed with sideboards you may want the quilt to reach only to the bottom of the boards, so measure to that point. If you want it to reach the floor, measure to the floor. For the sides, double this measurement and add to the width of the quilt. If, for example, your measurement is 14″, add 28″ to the width. Add 14″ to the length. In this instance, your finished quilt would measure:

Mattress size, double bed		54″ ×	75″
Allowance for pillows			18″
Overhang on each side, 14″		28″	
Overhang at foot, 14″			14″
		82″ ×	107″

Since most of your quilts will be made for the same beds, these measurements only need to be taken once, so that you have a general idea of the size you need.

14

For an all-over patchwork design with a binding or narrow border, the measurements aren't as critical and, of course, you can eliminate the pillow allowance if you just want to use the quilt as a cover rather than as a spread.

Do be flexible when it comes to the size of the quilt because too often the block size won't come out evenly to your measurements.

Using our example quilt, and an all-over design, check the chart, and you'll see some of the problems you'll have in matching block size to quilt size:

Desired size of quilt: 82" wide by 107" long. Your first adjustment could be to make it 106" long since no block size will come out to 107".

Block Size	Blocks Across	Blocks Down	Total Blocks Needed
8"	10 = 80"	13 = 104"	130
	2" border, or	3" border, or	
	9 = 72"	12 = 96"	108
	10" border	11" border	

(If you have reduced the size to 106, both of these will come out evenly.)

9"	9 = 81"	11 = 99"	99
	1" border	8" border, or	
	8 = 72"	11 = 99"	88
	10" border	8" border	

(There is too much of a discrepancy in the first example, but if you reduce the width by 2", the second example would work.)

10"	8 = 80"	10 = 100"	80
	2" border	7" border, or	
	7 = 70"	9 = 90"	63
	12" border	17" border	

(In both examples you have a 5" difference in the amount of border. The best solution is to use the first setting and omit the border.)

12"	6 = 72"	8 = 96"	48
	10" border	11" border	

(Same as 8" block.)

14"	5 = 70"	7 = 98"	35
	12" border	9" border	

(Increase the length by 3". This amount won't make that much difference on the pillow allowance.)

15"	5 = 75"	7 = 105"	35
	7" border	2" border	
	5 = 75"	6 = 90"	30
	7" border	17" border	

(Either omit borders, which eliminates the pillow allowance, or use another block size.)

Block Size	Blocks Across	Blocks Down	Total Blocks Needed
16″	5 = 80″ 2″ border	6 = 96″ 11″ border	30

(Omit borders, which eliminates pillow allowance, or use another block size.)

18″	4 = 72″ 10″ border	5 = 90″ 17″ border	20

(If 82″ is the absolute maximum width, cut both borders to 10″, but you won't have enough to cover the pillows. If you have evened the size to 106, you can't take any more away from the length; so you can only add to the width, if possible, or use another block size.)

Quilt Size: 82″ × 107″

Block Size	Blocks Across	Blocks Down	Total Blocks Needed
8″	8 = 64″ 7 2″ strips = 14″ 2″ border = 4″	11 = 88″ 9 2″ strips = 18″ 2″ border = 4″	88

Finished Size: 82″ × 110″

9″	7 = 63″ 6 2″ strips = 12″ 2″ border = 4″	9 = 81″ 8 2″ strips = 16″ 2″ border = 4″	63

Finished Size: 79″ × 101″

10″	6 = 60″ 5 3″ strips = 15″ 3″ border = 6″	8 = 80″ 7 3″ strips = 21″ 3″ border = 6″	48

Finished Size: 81″ × 107″

12″	5 = 60″ 4 3″ strips = 12″ 3″ border = 6″	7 = 84″ 6 3″ strips = 18″ 3″ border = 6″	35

Finished Size: 78″ × 108″

If you increase the borders to 4″, the finished size would be 80″ × 110″.

14″	5 = 70″ 4 2″ strips = 8″ 2″ border = 4″	7 = 98″ 5 2″ strips = 10″ 2″ border = 4″	35

Finished Size: 82″ × 112″

Block Size	Blocks Across	Blocks Down	Total Blocks Needed
15″	5 = 75″ 4 2″ strips = 8″ 2″ border = 4″	6 = 90″ 5 2″ strips = 10″ 2″ border = 4″	30

Finished Size: 87″ × 104″

16″	4 = 64″ 3 4″ strips = 12″ 4″ border = 8″	5 = 80″ 4 4″ strips = 16″ 4″ border = 8″	20

Finished Size: 84″ × 104″

18″	4 = 72″ 3 2″ strips = 6″ 2″ border = 4″	5 = 90″ 4 2″ strips = 8″ 2″ border = 4″	20

Finished Size: 82″ × 102″

Using 3″ strips:

3 3″ strips = 9″ 3″ border = 6″	4 3″ strips = 12″ 3″ border = 6″

Finished Size: 87″ × 108″

To determine the size of the blocks when set on the diagonal, you must multiply by 1.42. This figure is then divided into the desired size to determine how many blocks are needed.

The following chart shows the width of the block on the diagonal and how many blocks you need to make a quilt 82″ × 107″.

(rounded to nearest quarter inch)

8″ block = 11.36 or 11½″	7 = 80½″	9 = 103½″
9″ block = 12.78 or 12¾″	6 = 76½″	8 = 102″
10″ block = 14.2 or 14″	5 = 70″	7 = 98″
11″ block = 15.62 or 15½	5 = 77½″	6 = 93″
12″ block = 17.04 or 17″	4 = 68″	6 = 102″
13″ block = 18.46 or 18½	4 = 74″	5 = 92½
14″ block = 19.88 or 20″	4 = 80″	5 = 100″
15″ block = 21.3 or 21¼″	3 = 63¾″	5 = 106¼″
16″ block = 22.72 or 22¾″	3 = 68¼″	4 = 91″
17″ block = 24.14 or 24″	3 = 72″	4 = 96″
18″ block = 25.56 or 25½″	3 = 76½″	4 = 102″

Adjustments to reach the desired size are made the same as in the preceding charts. The number of blocks shown is the maximum possible, but you can subtract blocks and adjust the borders to come up to the proper size.

Once you have made a few quilts you will have a general idea of the size you like best. I like a quilt at least 84″ × 96″; so if I am using a 12″ block I know I'll need 56 blocks. As I mentioned earlier, the only time exact measurements are critical is when the design must fit the mattress top exactly.

ESTIMATING YARDAGE

Now that you have determined the quilt size and how many blocks are needed, you are ready to estimate how much fabric is needed. To illustrate, I'll use a simple nine-patch block of five dark and four light squares.

1. Total number of units per block for each color.
5 dark squares   4 light squares
2. Multiply by total number of blocks.
(9″ block; finished size 81″ × 99″; 99 blocks)

$$5 \times 99 = 495 \text{ dark squares}$$
$$4 \times 99 = 396 \text{ white squares}$$

3. Add seam allowance and measure each unit, both length and depth.
3″ squares + ½″ seam allowance on all sides =

$$4″ \text{ square}$$

4. Find the width on the accompanying chart. Go to the column titled Number of Units Across and find how many 4″ squares can be cut across the width of the fabric. In this case, 11.
5. Find the length under Number of Units Down. Since this is a square we again look for 4″. 9 pieces can be cut down the fabric length.
6. Multiply the number of units obtained in width by the number of units obtained in length to determine how many can be cut from 1 yard of fabric.

$$11 \times 9 = 99$$

7. Divide the total number of units needed by the number of units per yard to obtain total yardage required.

495 divided by 99 = 5 yards dark
396 divided by 99 = 4 yards white

Unit Size	Number of Units Across (45″ fabric)	Number of Units Down (36″ fabric)
1″	45	36
1½″	30	24
2″	22	18
2½″	18	14
3″	15	12
3½″	12	10
4″	11	9
4½″	10	8
5″	9	7
5½″	8	6
6″	7	6
6½″	6	5
7″	6	5

Unit Size	Number of Units Across (45″ fabric)	Number of Units Down (36″ fabric)
7½″	6	4
8″	5	4
8½	5	4
9″	4	4
9½″	4	3
10″	4	3
10½″	4	3
11″	4	3
12″	3	3
12½″	3	2

PATTERN DRAFTING

Most of the time, when you encounter a pattern you like, you use the pattern as is, making enough blocks to fit the bed on an approximate basis. However, if you visualize a pattern in a particular way, it may be necessary to change the pattern to another block size.

A sampler is the best example of when you might want to have blocks all the same size. If you have 9", 8", 12" and 15" patterns that you would like to use in a sampler, it's easy to make them all up as 12" blocks.

Years ago, ladies liked to use up all the tiny scraps they had and many designs were developed for this purpose. In some cases, though, they went too far. The *Kaleidoscope Quilt*, which appeared in the *Kansas City Star* in 1930, contains 133 pieces per block and is scaled to a 9" block! For a quilt measuring 63" × 72" you need 56 blocks for a total of 6,328 pieces, many of which are less than ½" in size.

Wouldn't it be much easier to double the size of the block to 18"?

The pieces would be of more manageable size and even though you would still need the same number of pieces per block, you would only need 16 blocks for a quilt 72" × 72".

The 12" block is generally the most popular size for a quilt block and most patterns are easily adapted to this size. However, the appearance of the pattern may call for a larger or smaller block. A simple nine-patch block scaled to 12" would give you individual squares of 4". Squares measuring 2" or 3" would give a better balance of color and design on the quilt top.

Once decided on the general size of the block, I scale the pattern to the nearest whole inch, or half-inch, depending on the block type. I will never use odd fractions such as three-eighths or two-thirds of an inch. To illustrate why: if you try to scale a nine-patch block to an 8" square, each segment equals 2⅔". Find that on a ruler! It's much easier to scale to a 9" block, making each segment equal to 3". If it must be smaller than 9", use 2" segments for a 6" block, or 1½" segments for a 7½" block.

You will need the following supplies to draft a pattern:

Graph Paper. The most common is four squares to the inch, but art suppliers and some office suppliers have it in two, four, five, six, eight and ten squares to the inch. This comes in 8½" × 11" tablets, but if you can find larger sheets,

21

buy them. You'll save a lot of time spent taping sheets together.

Pen or Pencil. A pen mark is easier to see, but a pencil allows you to make corrections. Make sure the pencil is sharp at all times.

Ruler—12″ and 18″. Try to get the see-through plastic type. These rulers have grid lines which allow you to make perfect squares and angles by lining up the markings on the ruler with your drawn lines. They are indispensable when drafting directly onto fabric.

Compass. This is needed for drawing circles. If the compass won't make as large a circle as needed, experiment with round items, such as plates or pan lids.

On the following pages are grids illustrating the various types of blocks along with the subdivisions most commonly used with each type.

Nine-Patch Patterns

Illus. 1. Square = Final block size.

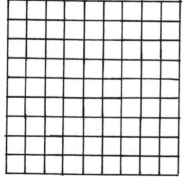

1″ = 3″ block	4″ = 12″ block
2″ = 6″ block	5″ = 15″ block
3″ = 9″ block	

Illus. 2. Divided in half = 6 squares.

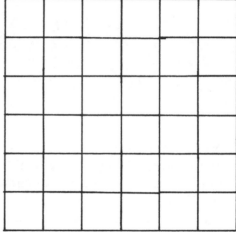

1″ = 6″ block	2½″ = 15″ block
1½″ = 9″ block	3″ = 18″ block
2″ = 12″ block	

Illus. 3. Divided in thirds = 9 squares.

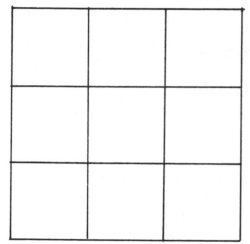

1″ = 9″ block
1½″ = 13½″ block
2″ = 18″ block

Illus. 4. Divided in fourths = 12 squares.

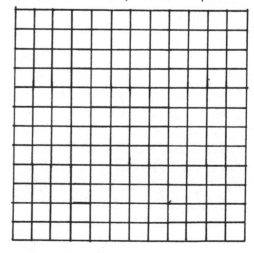

1″ = 12″ block
1½″ = 18″ block
2″ = 24″ block

Four-Patch Patterns

Illus. 5. Four-patch.

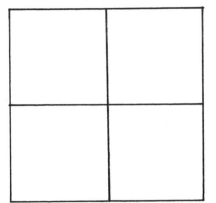

2″ = 4″ block   5″ = 10″ block
3″ = 6″ block   6″ = 12″ block
4″ = 8″ block

Illus. 6. Divided in half = 4 squares.

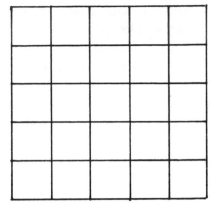

2″ = 8″ block   4″ = 16″ block
2½″ = 10″ block   4½″ = 18″ block
3″ = 12″ block   5″ = 20″ block
3½″ = 14″ block

Illus. 7. Divided in fourths = 8 squares.

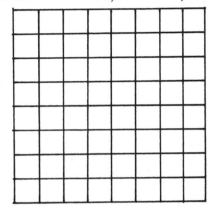

1″ = 8″ square
1½″ = 12″ square
2″ = 16″ square
2½″ = 20″ square
3″ = 24″ square

Five-Patch Patterns

Illus. 8. Five-patch.

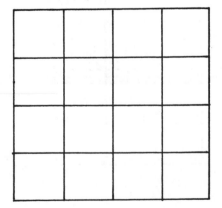

Illus. 9. Divided in half = 10 squares.

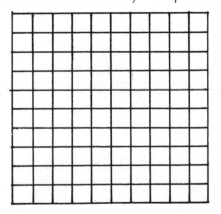

There are also a very few patterns based on a seven-patch division and an eleven-patch division.

The previous examples show only the basic squares. These, of course, can be further divided in numerous ways but once you can recognize how many squares make up a block, it is easy to determine the proportions of any further divisions within each square.

Once you have decided on the final block size, draw it full size on a sheet of graph paper. Divide it into the appropriate number of squares, nine, four, eight, or whatever. Now transfer any further dividing lines from your pattern to the full-size block.

Occasionally, you will encounter a pattern that is a combination of the patch types. The following nine-patch design combines a four-patch square with a nine-patch square. The final block size must be compatible with both patch types.

If we make the triangles 2″ the resulting square will equal 6″. The four-patch can be easily drawn in a 6″ square, giving a finished block size of 18″.

Illus. 10. Mother's Dream.

Illus. 11. 6″ square divided in half.

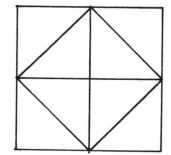

Illus. 12. 6″ square divided in thirds.

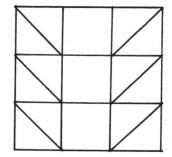

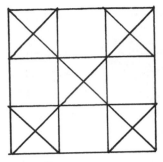

Illus. 13.

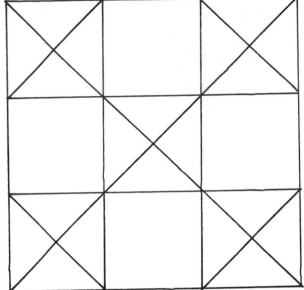

Illus. 14. Full-sized block.

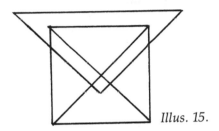

Illus. 15.

Many patterns, like the one given, are merely repeats of the same design elements throughout the block. In this instance, you really don't have to scale up a full-size block. In the above example, for a 12″ block, each square would equal 4″. Draw a 4″ square and add the diagonal lines to the square for a full-size pattern. Select one of the triangles and using your see-through ruler, lay the ½″ or ¼″ line along one of the edges. Draw in the seam allowance. Repeat for the other two sides.

Once you know the basic breakdown of patterns, it's a simple matter to design your own. Something as simple as changing the color placement within the design will create an entirely different effect.

Try experimenting a little. And the easiest way to do this is with pencil and paper. Draw one of your favorite pattern blocks on graph paper. Make a row of three or four, then add one or two more rows. Don't add any design or color to the drawing. Now stand back a little and look at the drawing. Without the color to restrict you, you should see at least one or two different ways the block could be worked.

The following drawings are of a quilt I saw on a friend's bed. It was quite old and worn and I have no idea what the name of the pattern is, but the drawings are a good example of the design process.

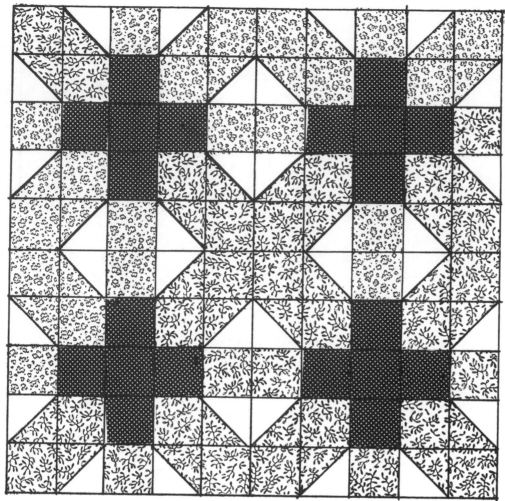

Illus. 16. The original quilt, showing four blocks.

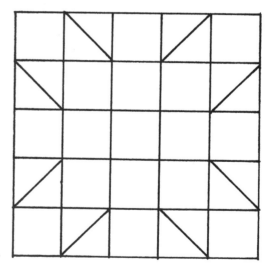

Illus. 17. The basic block.

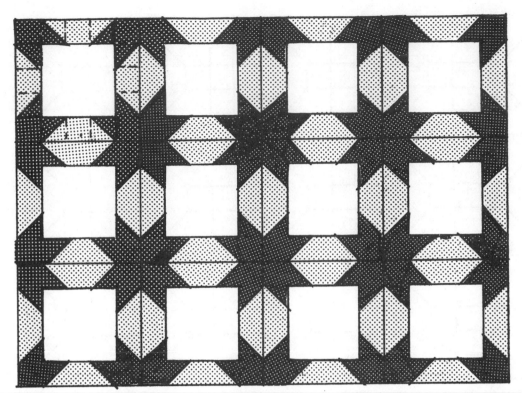

Illus. 18. A few line changes, a square takes the place of the center cross.

Illus. 19. This just kind of happened.

Illus. 20. This is only slightly different from the original. You could also change it by making the corner squares a different color.

Illus. 21. I was thinking here of either alternating light and dark squares or using lattice strips.

Before we get into sewing the patterns, a word should be said about matching seams. Perfectly matched seams begin with the pressing. Wherever two seams cross, press one seam to the left, the other to the right. Align the seams by sliding the two towards each other until they "nest" together.

When matching just one seam, pinning is not necessary since there will be little if any slippage, especially if you place the raw edges of the underside piece so that it faces you. In this way, you can keep the raw edge on top flat as it goes under the needle, and the one on the bottom will be fed through fold-first, which will keep it flat. If the raw edge on the bottom goes through first, it will often fold back on itself. It's not really a big problem, but if you like a neat back, this method will keep all the seams flat.

I should also mention grain line. Generally, the pattern pieces are cut so that the longest side of the pattern is cut on the lengthwise grain of the fabric. This is particularly true when cutting the outside edges of the block since this adds stability and prevents stretching along the edges. The crosswise grain can also be used, but it is second choice.

It is especially important that you cut all like pieces along the same grain line when using solid-color fabric. If you change the grain line from piece to piece, you will get slight shading differences when the pieces are sewn together.

Some of the methods presented here ignore the grain line, although all pieces are cut in the same direction. In some cases this will mean that the pieces are cut on the bias. Bias cuts tend to stretch or distort and care should be used when handling such pieces.

A pattern such as Lattice is traditionally cut on the bias but the pieces are then sewn to a foundation block as they are cut. The use of a very lightweight iron-on interfacing instead of the foundation block offers two advantages, although it does increase the cost. The interfacing stabilizes the fabrics to keep them from stretching and since it eliminates the bulk of the foundation block, the quilting is much easier.

UNIT-PIECING

Unit-piecing is a mass-production method that can be used for both traditional piecing and the shortcuts shown in this book, but is especially suitable for machine-sewing.

Instead of working on one block at a time, you assemble all like units of each block, feed-ing them continuously through the machine until you have completed them all. These small units are then sewn together to form larger units and finally into the complete block.

Following are two patterns which illustrate the process.

Pinwheel

1. Seam all A's to B's.
2. Seam all print and plain C's together.
3. Join AB's to C's.
4. Complete blocks.

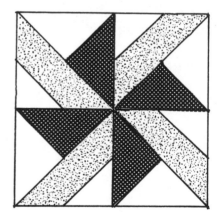

Illus. 22.

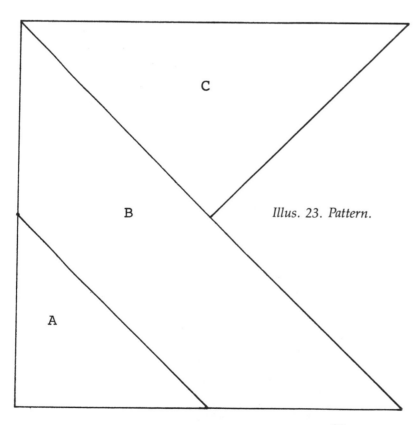

Illus. 23. Pattern.

Dove at the Window

Nine-patch design. Each square equals 4″ for a 12″ block.

Cut out all pieces. See sections on long triangles and quarter-square triangles.

Unit-Piecing

1. Seam an A to B triangle.
Seam second A to B.
2. If you have used the method shown under quarter-square triangles, your center square is complete.

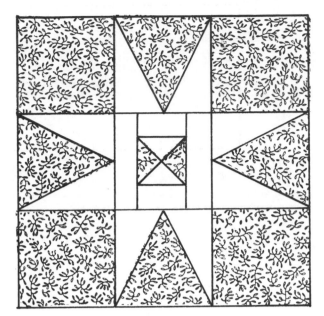

Illus. 24.

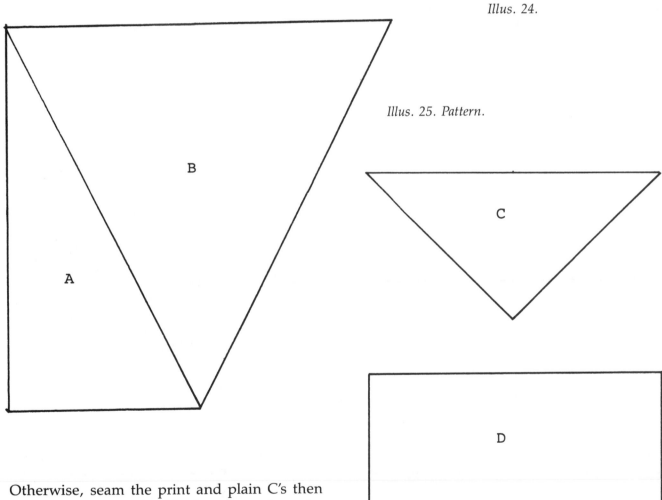

Illus. 25. Pattern.

Otherwise, seam the print and plain C's then join them across the block to complete the square.

3. Add D to top and bottom of center square.
4. Add E to sides of center square.

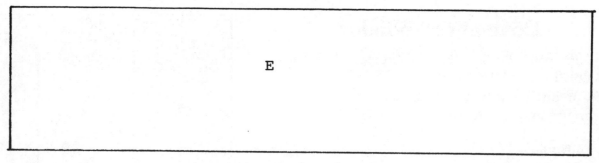

E

5. Assemble the completed squares into the block as shown.

F   *Corner Squares*

Illus. 25. (continued).

ADD SEAM ALLOWANCES

Kaleidoscope

This pattern can be grouped with either the nine-patch or four-patch blocks broken down into a twelve-patch each square = 1½″ for an 18″ block.

To assemble:

1. Construct half-square triangles.
2. Unit Piece: Add triangles to two edges of square.
Makes 8.
3. Assemble three of these large triangles with a plain one to form a square.
Make 8.
Follow diagram below for final assembly.

Illus. 26.

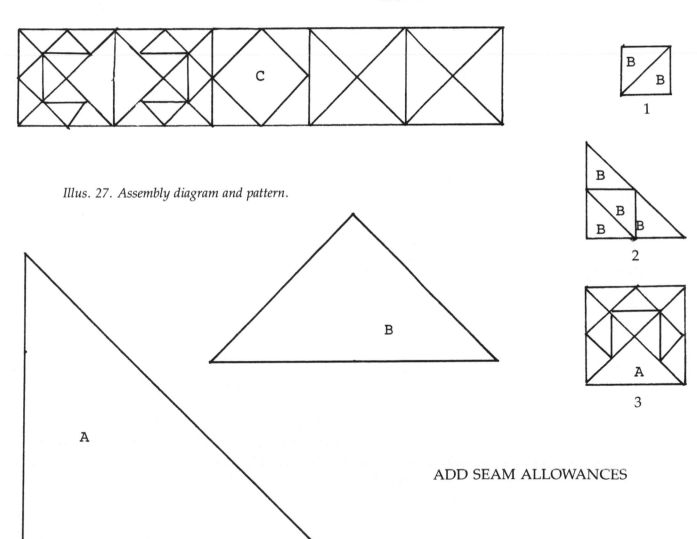

Illus. 27. Assembly diagram and pattern.

ADD SEAM ALLOWANCES

33

C

Illus. 27. (continued).

4. Assemble diagonally. This means units #3 and the center square are sewn to form one diagonal side of the pattern. Add A to each end to form corners.

5. Since the space between the two arms is all white, there is no reason to make this section three pieces. Just make it one large triangle. Base is 12″; depth is 6″.

6. Lay the assembled strip from step 4 in front of you. Sew a triangle; then add two unit 3's sewn together. Continue around with another triangle. Add A to the two #4 corners to complete the block.

TRIANGLES

Triangles are a common element in most quilt patterns. There are three types of triangles seen most often: the half-square triangle in which a square is divided diagonally across the square; the quarter-square triangle in which the square is divided diagonally both ways across the square; and what I call long triangles.

The half-square and quarter-square triangles are not difficult to sew into a square, but they do require a lot of time to mark and cut individually. The following method saves time, and when you cut out the patterns, you have a finished square, ready to set with any adjacent pieces.

Half-Square Triangles

Measure the straight edge of one side of the triangle; then add 1¾" for the seam allowance. The triangles are marked in squares, two per square, and the 1¾" allows a seam allowance for both triangles. If your triangle measures 3", you will draw a square 4¾". If it is 2", your square will be 3¾".

Iron your lightest color fabric and lay it on a large table. Use a straightedge and draw a straight guideline across the width of the fabric. Assume your triangle is 2", starting at one edge, mark the fabric across every 3¾". Lay your ruler lengthwise on the guideline, and measure

downwards 3¾". Draw in the squares. Lay your ruler diagonally from corner to corner of each square and mark. If you have a plastic transparent ruler, lay the ½" mark on the diagonal line and mark the seam line on both sides of the diagonal line.

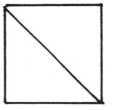

Illus. 28. Half-square triangle.

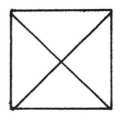

Illus. 29. Quarter-square triangle.

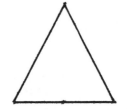

Illus. 30. Long triangle.

Once you have the fabric marked, lay it on top of the darker fabric, right sides together. To prevent shifting as you sew, place a pin in each triangle. Sew all the seams, stopping at the edge of each square. Do not sew through the points to the next block. Cut out the completed squares on the solid lines.

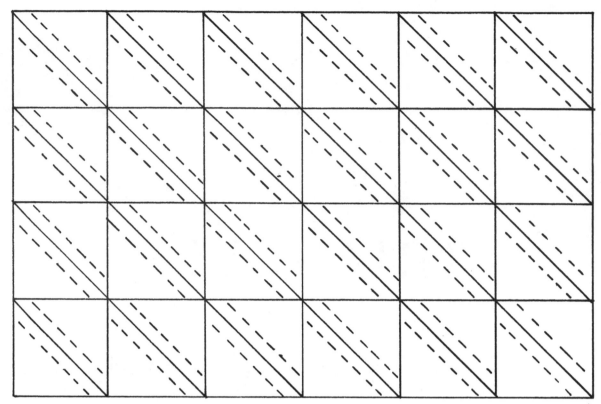

Illus. 31. Half-square triangles.

Quarter-Square Triangles

The procedure for making quarter-square triangles is basically the same as for half-square triangles. Measure the base of the triangle and add 2½″ to obtain the size of the square needed, in this case 5½″. Draw the squares on the lighter fabric just as you did for the half-square triangles. This time you draw diagonal lines both ways on the square.

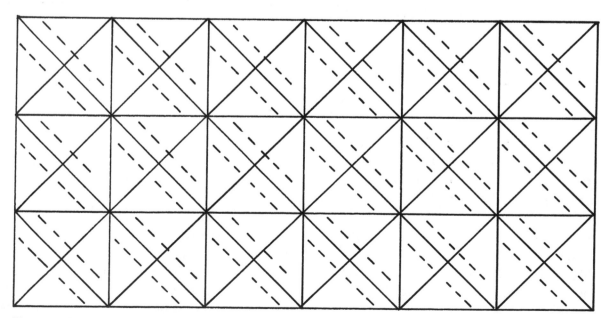

Illus. 32. Quarter-square triangles.

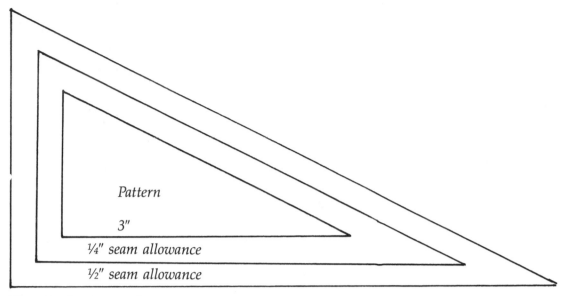

Illus. 33. Cutting template.

Pattern

3″

¼″ seam allowance

½″ seam allowance

The two sewn triangles will form a half-square triangle, which must be matched with another half-square and sewn together. Each square will yield four triangles or half-squares, which when sewn together will give you two complete squares.

Keep in mind that you must have a right and left side to form the square; so be careful when sewing that all the triangles don't come out the same. To avoid confusion, mark the seam line along both sides of one diagonal line. You can sew through the crossing diagonal, but again, stop at the edge of the square, lift the needle and begin stitching within the next square.

Long Triangles

Long triangles have two undesirable characteristics, the first being that when you add a ½″ seam allowance you use a piece of fabric almost twice the size needed. Even if you use a ¼″ seam allowance, a 3″ triangle uses a piece of fabric 4½″ long.

The second problem is caused by this excess fabric. You cannot just lay the two diagonal edges together and sew them because the tri-

angles won't match properly and the edges of the finished rectangle will not be straight. Even if you spend the time marking each seam line and matching the seams accurately, the edges still may not be perfectly straight when sewn.

The following cutting method solves both problems by eliminating the excess material before the fabric is cut. The two diagonal edges can be sewn together without marking. The triangles will match properly and the finished edges of the rectangles will be straight.

1. Measure length and width of triangle seam line.
2. Add 2″ to width (includes ½″ seam allowance). Add 1″ to length (includes ½″ seam allowance).
3. Draw a rectangle using these measurements.
4. Measure in ¾″ from the top right corner and ¾″ from the left lower corner and mark. Draw a line connecting the two marks. This is the cutting line.

Draw several rows of rectangles across the width of your fabric. Stack several layers of fabric, lay the marked fabric on top and cut out.

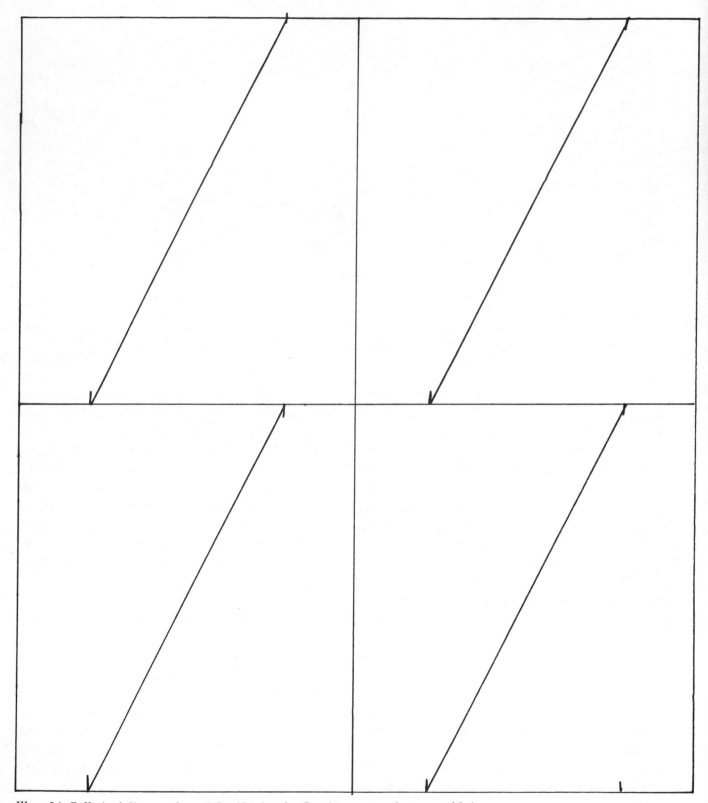

Illus. 34. Full-sized diagram for a 1½″ × 3″ triangle. Continue rectangles across fabric.

PATTERNS

Thorny Thicket

Four-patch divided into eight 2″ squares making a 16″ block.
Strip-piece center squares.
Mark and cut long triangles.
Make templates for corner squares, cutting off points.

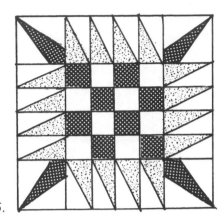

Illus. 35.

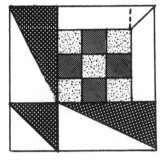

Illus. 36.

Bouquet and Fan

Nine-patch divided into six 2″ squares making a 12″ block.
Strip-piece center squares.
Mark and cut long triangles.
Mark, sew and cut half-square triangles.
Convert corner pieces into two straight pieces.

Storm at Sea

This pattern uses long triangles and they can be cut out as described. However, you have several other pieces that will also have too much fabric for easy matching once the seam allowance is added. In these cases, you can eliminate the excess by modifying the template as follows:

1. On a sheet of paper, draw the full-size pattern; then add seam allowance.

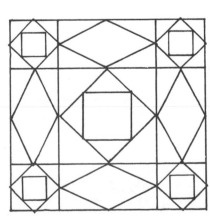

Illus. 37.

2. Lay the two paper patterns together, matching seam lines. Cut off any areas that go beyond the seam allowance as shown by the dark areas in the drawings.

3. You can either paste these modified paper patterns onto cardboard or plastic or redraw them as modified onto sturdy template material.

Now the pieces can be joined along the edges without marking or pinning.

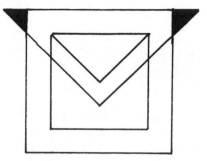

Illus. 38.

Illus. 39.

40

STRIP-PIECING

The uses of strip-piecing run the gamut of patchwork design, from a simple nine-patch block to the elaborate designs of the Seminole Indians. Its uses are constantly being expanded and once you are familiar with it, I'm sure you too will find more and more patterns that can be adapted to this method.

Basically, strip-piecing is the sewing together of fabrics in a planned order to form a new fabric, which is then cut apart to form sections of a quilt block.

We'll start with the simplest of shapes, a rectangle, to illustrate the fundamentals of strip-piecing. There are numerous patterns which use this simple shape, and there are seemingly endless ways to turn the strips to create new designs.

When strip-piecing, you can use either a ¼" or a ½" seam allowance. I personally prefer the ½". I've found that if I use less than this, the fabric will get caught in the feed dog when I start sewing the seam.

PATTERNS

Endless Stair

Illus. 40.

For our first exercise we will make the pattern *Endless Stair*. Our finished rectangle will measure 2" × 4".

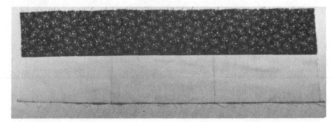

Illus. 41.

1. Choose two sharply contrasting fabrics and press them well. Lay the lighter of the two fabrics on a large flat surface and, using a straight-

edge, even off the end so that it is straight. It is not necessary to open the fabric out; just mark it folded as it comes from the bolt.

2. Measure down from the straightedge 3″. Make several marks across the fabric, then draw a line joining the marks. This includes a ½″ seam allowance. Draw several rows of 3″ wide strips.

3. Lay the darker fabric under the marked fabric and pin each row to be sure they stay even.

4. Using scissors or a rotary cutter, cut out the strips and sew them together. Press seams towards the darker fabric.

5. Lay a strip crosswise in front of you; measure and mark every 5″. Stack several strips, lining up the seams. Place the marked strip on top, pinning to secure. Cut strips apart.

6. Sew the units together, starting with dark at the top crosswise, then add one lengthwise with dark next to the previous unit. Continue alternating across in rows until you reach the size needed.

Pinwheel Squares

This pattern is made from the two strips of *Endless Stair*. There is another version in the back.

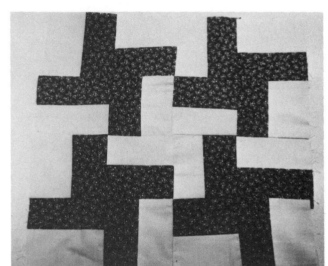

Illus. 42.

Basket Weave

If we add another 3″ strip and change the dimensions of the rectangle to 2″ × 6″ (3″ × 7″ with seam allowance) we can make the pattern shown in Illus. 43.

Illus. 43.

42

Spirit of St. Louis

Add one more strip and cut the strips at 9" intervals, finished size 2" × 8", and you have the block for *Rail Fence* (Illus. 45).

All of these designs can be done as a scrap quilt, with one fabric used throughout to bring out the focal point of the design.

Illus. 44.

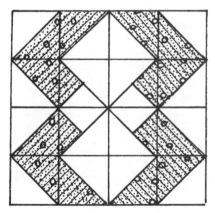

Illus. 45.

Rail Fence

In this pattern you can use both the half-square triangle and the quarter-square triangle method.

Squares

Almost every design has squares in it somewhere, so it is really a time-saver to be able to strip-sew these units.

First, of course, you must decide on the size of the block, so you can determine what size the squares will be. In the first example, a simple nine-patch, we'll deal with only how to strip-piece to achieve a nine-patch block, so we'll use an arbitrary size of 2". This makes a 6" square, which can later be combined with alternate 6" plain blocks to form a *Single Irish Chain* or with numerous other settings to form other blocks.

Nine-Patch

1. Select two contrasting fabrics. For 2″ squares, we must add 1″ for the seam allowance, so cut strips 3″ wide. You will need three dark and three light strips.

2. Seam them together, using a ½″ seam allowance, in the following order: Strip 1: dark, light, dark. Strip 2: light, dark, light.

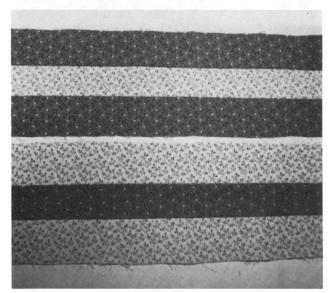

Illus. 47.

3. Press the strips. Measure and mark the length of the strip every 3″. You can mark one strip, then stack other strips under it, pin and then cut apart.

4. Sew these completed sections in the proper order to form the nine-patch.

Illus. 46.

Any number of colors or strips can be added as needed. Strips of scraps can be sewn together in long widths, even as wide as the finished quilt top, if desired, then cut apart and reassembled by turning the strips in each row.

By combining squares and rectangles, you have a whole new series of patterns to make.

Illus. 48.

Double Irish Chain

Two blocks make up this design, each one measuring 10″ so each square of the block measures 2″.

For block one you need three strips made up of five 3″ wide lengths of fabric.

The second block is made up of squares and rectangles. Make a strip using 3″ wide strips of dark set on each side of a 7″ wide light strip. For the center, cut a light strip 7″ wide.

Measure and mark the five strip-pieces at 3″ intervals and cut apart. Mark the square, rectangle pieces at 3″ intervals and cut. Measure

Illus. 49.

and cut the center strip at 11″ intervals. Sew these units together in the order shown in the finished block.

Tick-Tack-Toe

This is a nine-patch block; each major square equals 4″ for a 12″ block. To start, you need two assembled strips. Strip 1: Cut two strips dark fabric 2″ wide, one strip print fabric, 3″ wide. Sew these with the print between the two dark fabrics. Press. Measure and cut every 2″.

Illus. 50.

Illus. 51.

Strip 2. Two strips print fabric, 2″ wide, one strip plain fabric 3″ wide. Sew the print strips to each side of the plain. Mark and cut this strip every 4″. Cut one piece 3″ long for the center of each block.

To complete the block you need four 5″ squares.

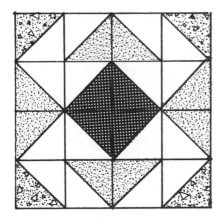

Illus. 52.

Mosaic No. 1

This is another pattern made up of unequal triangles, but if you follow the grid lines, you will see that this too can be converted to half-square triangle construction.

Autumn Tints

This is a super-easy pattern that makes up into a rather striking quilt.

Select a print fabric for the large squares. These are supposed to be the same color throughout, but I ran out of the brown print; so I arranged the greenish print around the edge. Cut the print into 7″ squares.

For the small squares, cut a print and plain fabric into 4″ strips and seam together. The plain should be the same throughout, but the prints can be scraps. I had enough of each one to follow the stairstep design all the way across, but if you don't, just keep them the same value in each diagonal row. Cut the seamed strips apart every 4″, then sew them back together in a checkerboard fashion.

To set the quilt, start with a pieced square, alternate a plain, then a pieced, across the row. Start the second row with a plain square and so on. Position the pieced squares so that the prints form a diagonal pattern across the quilt.

For the border, I cut 3″ wide strips and seamed them together until I had a piece of "fabric" about a yard wide. I then cut this "fabric" at 6″ intervals, seaming the 6″ wide strips together as necessary to go around the quilt.

Illus. 53.

This quilt-top can be completed in about eight hours.

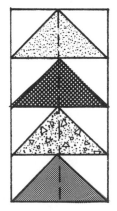

Illus. 54.

Flying Geese

This is a simple two-patch design, but you do run into the problem of matching triangles and making them come out even. You can modify the templates as shown with the *Storm at Sea* pattern, but an even easier, faster way is to change the pattern itself. If you draw a line down the center of the *Flying Geese* strip, you will see two half-square triangles. By converting to half-square triangles, you can use that method for sewing the triangles, then match them at the center and run them through the machine, one after the other.

Four Crosses

Illus. 55. Original pattern.

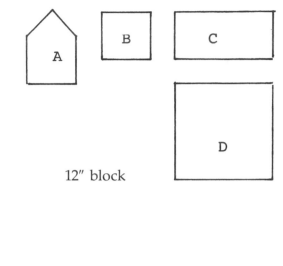

A   B   C

D

12″ block

(measurements include seam allowance)

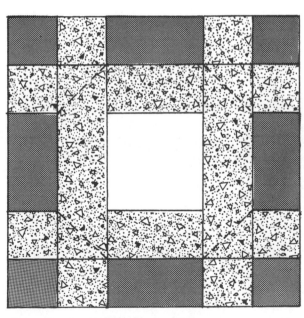

Illus. 56. Simplified for strip-piecing.

3″   3″   5″

Swastika

A four-patch design, if scaled to a 12″ square, each section of the grid is 1½″. The first strip is cut 2½″ wide. The second section is color and white, each strip cut 4″ wide. The third strip is three pieces, color 4″ wide, white 2½″ wide, and dark 2½″ wide.

Cutting the strips apart: Cut the print strip 7″ long; mark across the color and white strip every 4″ and cut apart; the third strip is cut across the three colors to measure 2½″ wide.

Assemble each section according to the diagram.

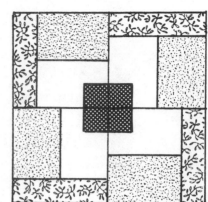

Illus. 57.

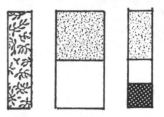

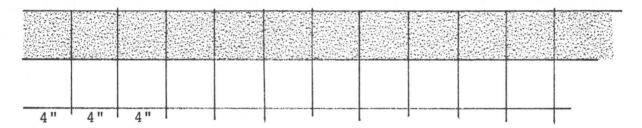

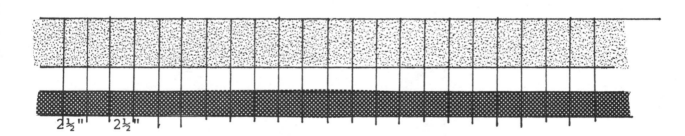

Leavenworth

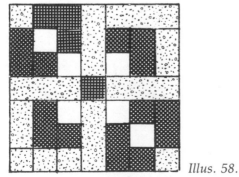

Illus. 58.

Seven-Patch

Stonemason's Puzzle

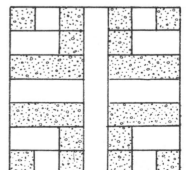

Illus. 59.

Seven-Patch

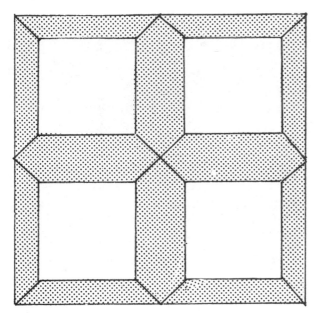

Illus. 60. Original version.

Shepherd's Crossing

A 12″ block. The original version contains angled pieces framing a set-in square.

The revised version contains all straight lines which can be strip-pieced following the piecing diagram. The diagonal lines of the design can be shown in the quilting, if desired.

Illus. 62. Piecing diagram. (Finished size, add seam allowance to measurements.)

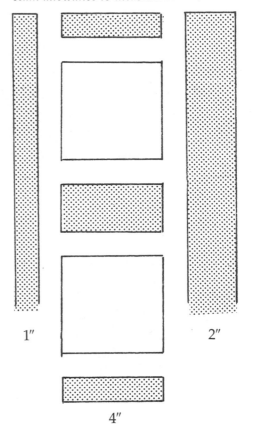

1″   2″

4″

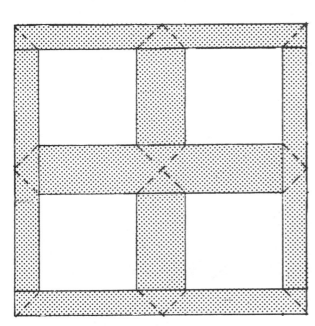

Illus. 61. Revised version.

49

King's Crown

This is a five-patch pattern; each square equals 2" for a 10" block. Fabrics are cut and sewn into strips as shown in Illus. 64.

1. 3" wide dark, 9" wide medium
2. 3" dark, 3" medium, 3" plain, 3" medium
3. 3" dark, 5" medium
4. 3" dark, 3" medium
5. 3" wide dark strip

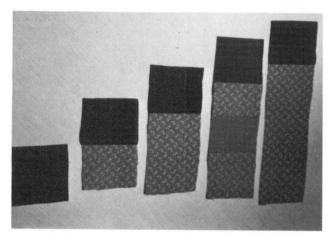

Illus. 64.

Press strips and cut apart at 3" intervals. Reassemble as shown, staggering the strips 2" as each is added. Press.

Place the completed half-block in front of you and lay a straightedge across the diagonal edge, allowing a ½" seam allowance from the point where the seams cross. Draw a line; then cut along this line. Half the block is now finished. Several half-blocks can be made from the assembled strips.

Illus. 63.

To draft the pattern for the second half of the block, see Illus. 65.

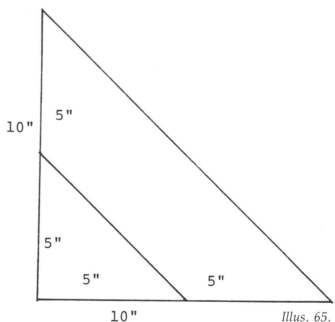

Illus. 65.

Attic Window

This pattern forms a three-dimensional image by the juxtaposition of light, dark and medium fabrics. In its original form, it is a fairly simple pattern to piece, except for the set-in of the square piece. This can be eliminated by making a half-square triangle of each color to form a square, then sewing this square to one of the side pieces for all straight-line sewing. But you still have to mark and cut all those pieces. The method below saves you the time of marking and cutting by strip-piecing the entire block.

This method requires two strips of fabric, which are then cut apart to form a half-square triangle.

Strip 1: Cut dark fabric 2½" wide. Cut light fabric 3½" wide. Sew together.

Strip 2: Cut medium fabric 2½" wide and light fabric 3½" wide. Sew together.

Illus. 66.

The one drawback to this method is that it does waste fabric since the triangles must go in one direction. However, if you have nothing against working on two quilts at once, the cut-off pieces can be used for a second quilt.

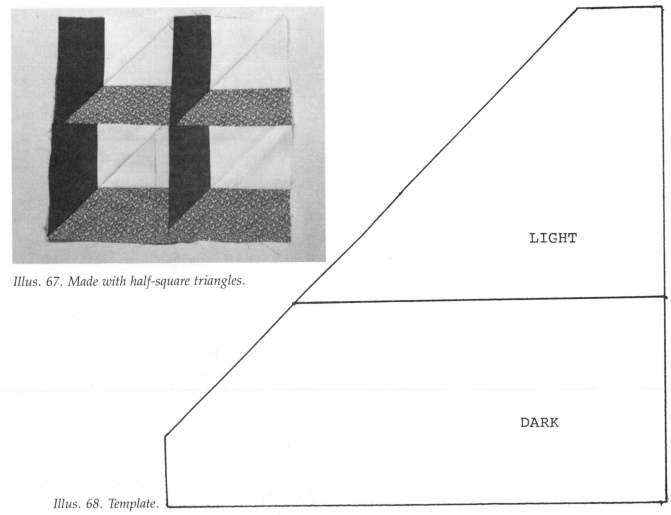

Illus. 67. Made with half-square triangles.

LIGHT

DARK

Illus. 68. Template.

51

After pressing, lay one of the strips in front of you and position the template with the crossline on the seam line. Mark around and cut out the half-square triangles. (The points of the template have been squared off.) On the other strip, turn the template over to the reverse side and mark around it as before. Sew the two triangles together to form a 4″ block.

I called this version *Peacock Eyes*, but in about five minutes I had formed seven other possible patterns.

Illus. 69. Peacock Eyes.

Lattice

Illus. 70.

This is another scrap quilt that can be strip-pieced, saving many hours of marking and cutting. In fact, you could use a combination of strip-piecing and traditional piecing, depending on the scraps you have on hand. Use the long strips for strip-piecing; then utilize smaller pieces in the traditional manner.

Each square of the block measures 6″. Four squares are set together, forming a 12″ block with an X in the middle of the block. These four blocks are then set with a lattice strip to another 12″ block, and four of these blocks are then set with another lattice strip to another set of four.

The strips can vary in width except for the one that runs through the middle of each block. This should be the same color and width in order to form the X in each block. This X can be a different color in each block, but the strip should remain the same width. All other strips can be whatever width or color, even within the same block.

Traditionally, this pattern is constructed on a foundation block since all the pieces are set on the bias. You must be very careful not to stretch the edges. This would be a good place to use iron-on interfacing to help stabilize the fabrics. It's not absolutely necessary if you're careful, but it does make it easier.

Cut a strip for the center 3″ wide, being sure it is long enough to cut four blocks. Add strips to each side until the "fabric" measures 9½″ to 10″ wide. If a strip runs short, just add on to it, using either the same or a different fabric. If the fabric is the same, the seam won't show, but if it is a different color, you might want to skip over the seam in placing the template.

Cut out a 7″ square template. Draw a guideline down the exact center of the center strip for placing the template.

Turn the template so it is on the diagonal and lay the top and bottom points along the guideline you drew. Draw around the template. Cut out the squares.

Cut 3″ wide strips from a light fabric. This will give a 2″ wide lattice strip, and the same fabric will be used throughout. At this time, also select a dark fabric for the outer lattice strips. From this fabric, cut 3″ squares for the intersection of the light lattice strips. From the light fabric you should also cut 4″ squares for the intersection of the dark lattice strips.

The dark strips should be cut 4″ wide. These are used to join the four-block and lattice-strip units.

When I made the sample blocks for this quilt, I used the leftover strips from the border of *Autumn* as a starting point. This was a fairly wide strip, so I started on one side, selecting a strip for the center, then moved the template to a new set of strips. I just kept adding strips on as I ran out.

Once the squares are cut, you will find a fairly large triangle left over. These triangles can be used to make another quilt as I mentioned under *Attic Windows*. Following are a few of the possible patterns.

Illus. 71.

Illus. 73.

Illus. 72.

Sunshine and Shadows

This Amish design is usually done as a scrap pattern, but you can also coordinate the colors. The picture of this quilt was made from a striped fabric, which made it really quick to complete. The finished blocks were then set on the diagonal for a slightly different look.

If using the strip-piecing method, it would be best to make this a scrap quilt so that all the fabric can be used, since this method will create two patterns of the strips.

Illus. 74.

1. Determine the finished size of the block. I'll use a 12″ block for illustration. Make up a template to this size, adding seam allowance. In this case I would draw a half-square triangle measuring 12″ on a side. Add the seam allowance; then cut out the template.

2. Making the fabric: The strips can be any width desired, but 1½″ to 2″ wide would allow for a lot of color. If I make the strips 2″ wide, I can utilize six different fabrics. Adding the seam allowance, cut the strips 3″ wide. Seam them together to form a "fabric" 13″ wide.

3. Lay the template on the completed strip and draw around it. Turn the template over and line it up with the diagonal line just drawn. This creates a reverse placement of the colors. Con-

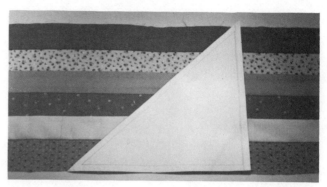

Illus. 75.

tinue marking down the strip. Cut out along the marked lines.

4. From a dark solid fabric, cut triangles using the template from above. Sew these two sections together to form the block.

Spider Web ·

There are several versions of this design, many of which can be adapted to strip-piecing. This is usually made up as a scrap pattern, the only restriction being that the same fabric be used within each block.

In this version, the hexagons are set together with a plain white triangle. To square off the quilt, cut the template in half through the point and add a seam allowance to the cut edge.

Any number of fabrics can be used to form the *Spider Web*. I've used three, the third of which forms a smaller solid band within the larger hexagon. If an even number of strips are used, you will get an alternating pattern between the segments.

If using three fabrics, cut three strips 3″ wide.

If using four fabrics, cut each strip 2½″ wide. Seam the strips together to form your "fabric."

Lay the pressed fabric in front of you and lay the template at one corner. Trace around it. Turn the template upside down and lay it along the line just drawn. Be sure the points are even. Trace around the template again. Continue across the fabric strip. Cut out the triangles.

Sew two sets of three triangles together, alternating light and dark. Sew the two sets of

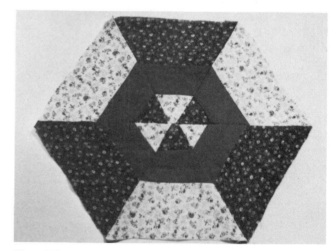

Illus. 76.

three together across the middle. To make the final assembly easier, begin sewing each of the segments ½″ in from the point at the center, sewing towards the outside edge.

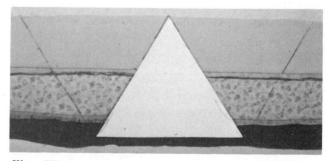

Illus. 77.

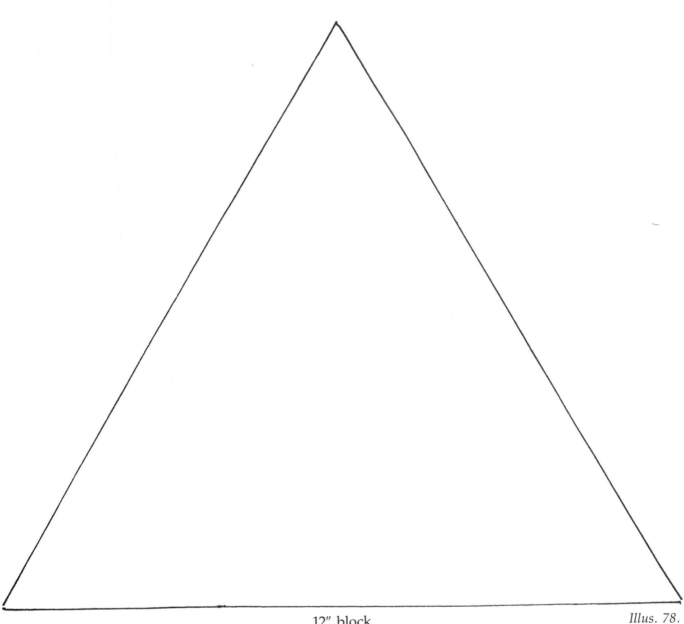

12" block

Illus. 78.

Casement Window

This is the type of pattern in which Seminole piecing works to best advantage. You should be able to sew up four to six blocks in about an hour.

This block has a center strip, then four identical strips on each side. Start with the center strip, working diagonally across the block to prepare your strips.

Illus. 79.

55

Center Strip: 3" blue, 3" white, 3" red, 7" blue, 3" red, 3" white, 3" blue
Seam together in this order.
Row 1: 3" blue, 3" red, 3" white, 3" blue, 3" white, 3" red, 3" blue
Row 2: 3" blue, 7" red, 3" blue
Row 3: 3" blue, 3" white, 3" blue
Row 4: 3" blue

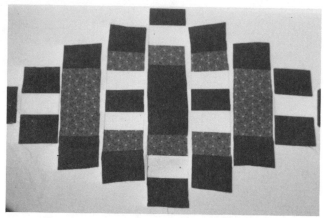

Illus. 80.

Lay the center strip out flat and measure 3" from one end, straightening the end if necessary. Cut out the strip.

Cut two 3" wide strips from the remaining sets. This will make one block.

Lay the center strip out and position the other strips on each side of the center. The rows will be staggered. Match seams and sew the strips together.

Illus. 81.

To even off the edge, lay your plastic transparent ruler with the ½" line on the points of the red and white squares. Mark. Cut off along the line drawn.

DRAFTING
DIAMONDS

So many patterns use diamond shapes that it is a good idea to know how to draft one to the size you want. I don't care how many patterns you have for diamonds, the one you need is never there.

Determine the size diamond you need and cut out a square of graph paper twice this size. This is measuring the side edges of the diamond. For a diamond that's 3″ on a side, I need a 6″ square.

Draw a line diagonally across the square. Measure along the diagonal line 3″ and mark. Cut to this mark. Fold the cut edge straight up. Draw around the triangle.

Draw a straight line across the square touching the top point of the diamond. Draw in the adjacent diamond, which will give you the corner square.

For your convenience, on the following pages are several sizes of both 45° and 60° diamonds, plus hexagons.

Another way to arrive at the size pattern needed is to choose one of the patterns closest to the size you need, then using your plastic transparent ruler, lay the line of the ruler on the line of the pattern and increase or decrease. In other words, if you need a pattern ½″ larger than the largest diamond, lay the ½″ mark on the ruler along the lines of the pattern and draw a new diamond.

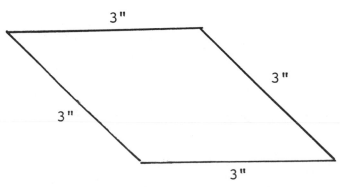

Illus. 82. 45° diamond for making an 8-point star.

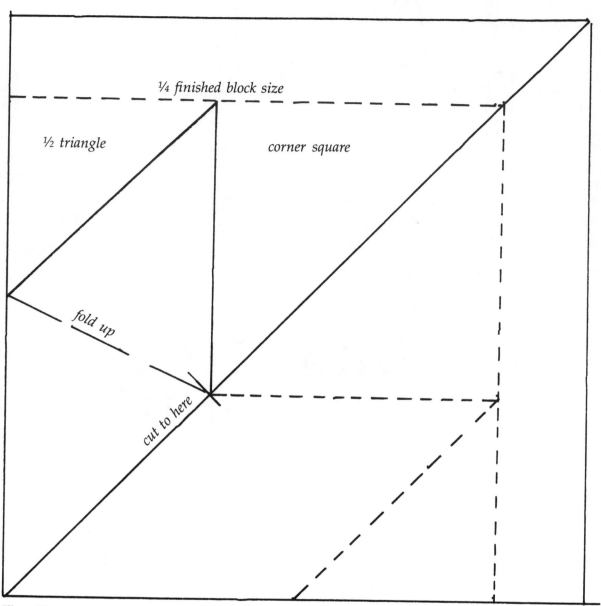

¼ finished block size

½ triangle

corner square

fold up

cut to here

Illus. 83.

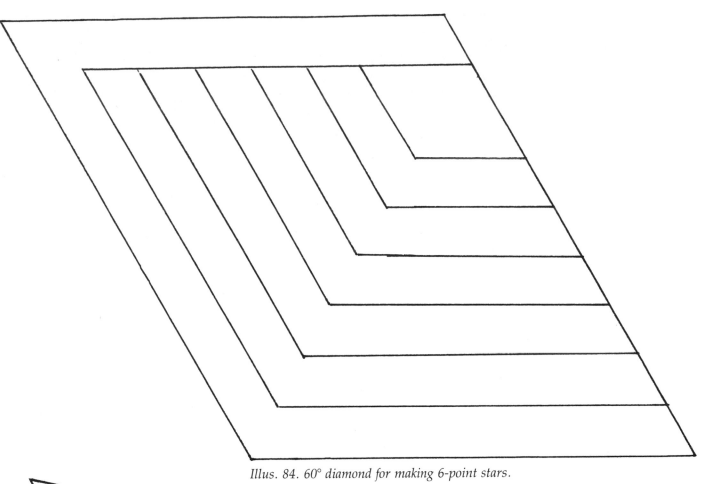

Illus. 84. 60° diamond for making 6-point stars.

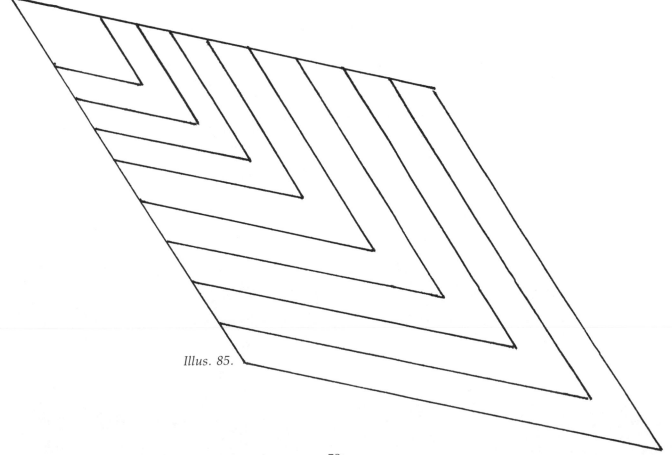

Illus. 85.

59

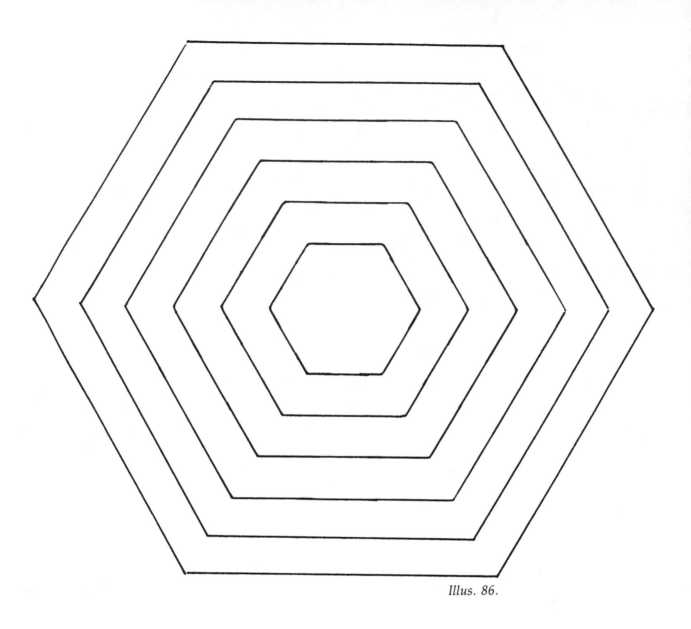

Illus. 86.

HOW TO SEW DIAMOND STARS

Two problem areas occur when sewing an eight-point star. The first is that all seams meet at the center, creating a very bulky area, which, in turn, causes the second problem: The star won't lie flat.

With proper care during construction, both of these problems can be alleviated.

Mark both the cutting line and the seam line on the fabric. Sew four sets of two diamonds together, beginning and ending exactly on the seam line. Do not go beyond the seam line.

1. Sew two of these together, beginning and ending on seam line, to form half of the star. Repeat with other two units.

Illus. 87.

3. Press this final seam open, fanning the ends of the diamonds to lessen the bulk at the center.

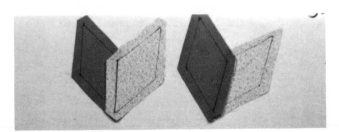

Illus. 88.

2. Join these two half-stars together in a continuous seam to complete the star.

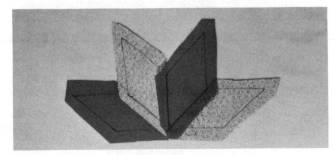

Illus. 89.

SEWING SET-IN
PIECES

A set-in piece is one that must be joined to two edges, as in the triangle and corner squares of an eight-point star.

Using the star as an example, sew the diamond as shown. Mark seam lines on all pieces to be joined. Take the corner square and line up the seam lines of the square and the diamond, right sides together. Pin. Begin at the outside edge and stitch along the seam line, ending stitching exactly at the end of the seam line. *Do not take one stitch into the seam allowance.* Remove the piece from the machine and pin the other side of the square in place. Sew as before, from the outside edge to the end of the seam line.

Although this may seem to take a bit longer than pivoting or turning the piece on the needle, in the long run it will save you time. Often when you pivot the needle, you will catch a fold in the fabric, or a stitch will go too far into the seam allowance, causing a pucker on the surface which then must be ripped out and redone. If you use the above method exactly as described you will never have to rip out a seam and redo it.

An alternative to sewing set-in pieces is to change the pattern so that there aren't any. This will require more cutting time, but the sewing will be all straight-line sewing, which will go faster and be more accurate.

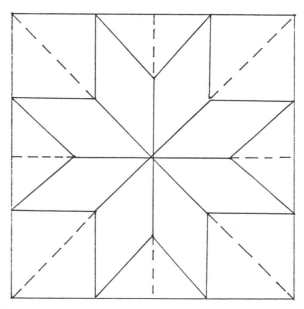

Illus. 90.

In the example of the eight-point star, you can change the pattern as shown.

Cut the square and triangle pieces in half as indicated by the dashed line. Remember to add seam allowances to these new pieces. Sew these new pieces to each side of the diamonds.

When you sew the diamonds together, sew from the outside edge using a straight seam, stopping at the end of the seam line as before.

PIECING
THE LONE STAR

The *Lone Star* pattern is probably one of the top five in popularity, especially among more experienced quilters. It is also an extremely time-consuming pattern to piece because of the large number of diamond shapes that must be joined together. The example given here contains 392 diamonds, but many quilts have several hundred more to make up the final star, which could take months of piecing. Using the strip-piecing method, I completed the star given here in approximately 20 hours.

Even using this method, the beginner probably should not make this a first or second project, but it takes just a small bit of experience to achieve good results. As in all quilting, the main watchword is accuracy. Step-by-step instructions follow to help you complete your spectacular *Lone Star*.

1. Lay out the fabric in color sequence.
2. Either number the fabrics or use an abbreviation to fill in the layout chart to help you keep the colors in proper sequence.
3. Make a template of the diamond, being sure

Illus. 91.

to include a ½″ seam allowance. The pattern given is cutting size.
4. At this point you establish the cutting width of the strips. Measure the height of the diamond which tells you how wide the strips should be. A second method is to lay the template on the fabric as shown in Illus. 94, and

64

draw a straight line across the width of the cloth, even with the bottom edge of the template. This eliminates measuring.

5. Cut out the strips. In this example, one strip in each combination of rows will be enough for

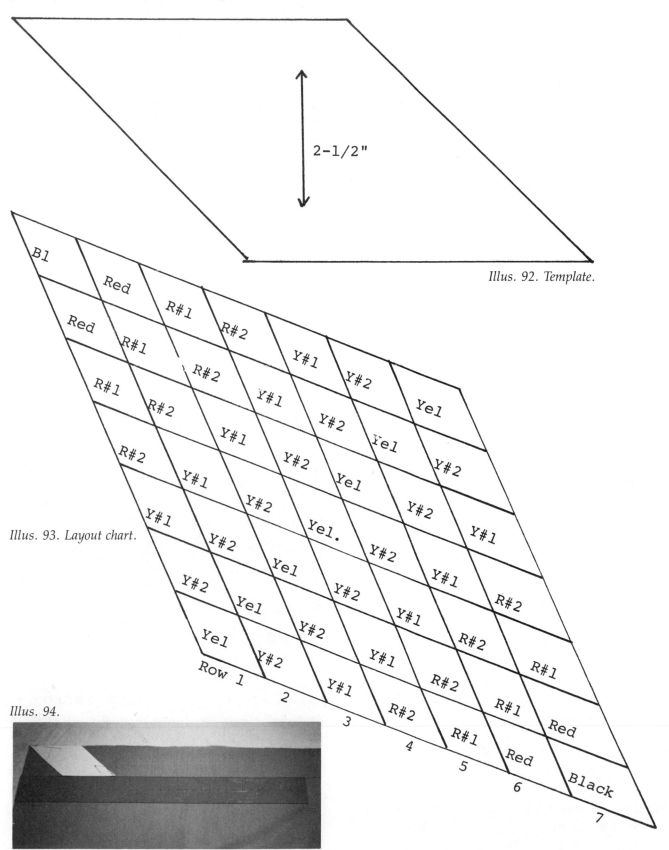

2-1/2"

Illus. 92. Template.

Illus. 93. Layout chart.

B1
Red
Red
R#1
R#1
R#1
R#2
R#2
R#2
R#2
Y#1
Y#1
Y#1
Y#1
Y#2
Y#2
Y#2
Y#2
Yel
Yel
Yel
Yel.
Yel
Yel
Y#2
Y#2
Y#1
Y#2
Y#1
Y#2
Y#1
Y#1
R#2
R#2
R#1
R#2
R#1
R#1
Red
Red
Black

Row 1
2
3
4
5
6
7

Illus. 94.

65

all eight points of the diamond. Following your layout, cut strips for each row.

6. Press strips. On each strip, measure in 2½" and mark.

7. Lay out strips in proper color sequence, beginning with #1 at the bottom and ending with #7 at the top.

8. Take strips #1 and #2. Place edge of #2 at marked line on #1, right sides together. Stitch. The edge of strip #3 is lined up with marked line of #2 and sewn. This staggering of the strips eliminates a lot of wasted fabric.

Note: Since accuracy is of the utmost importance when working with diamonds, it is important that the seams be absolutely true. The very nature of fabric makes it difficult to ensure accuracy. The cloth may stretch some in marking, or maybe the cut strips are not all the same width. If there is enough room on the strip to sew a seam, you won't have to redo the strip.

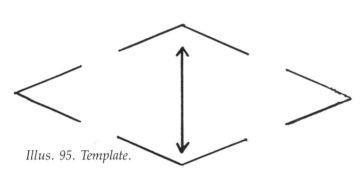

Illus. 95. Template.

Sew the first two strips together. To determine the exact amount of fabric that should be between the seams, measure the finish size of the diamond crosswise from point to point. If using the pattern given, it should be 1½". Before joining the next strip, lay your ruler across the strip with the end against the seam. Measure off 1½" or the width required, and mark. Do this down the strip as you sew, adjusting the seam as needed.

9. Press seams of completed strips to one side.

10. Now we'll make a template for cutting the strips apart. Spread out a sheet of newspaper and draw a straight line across the top. Lay the template along this straight line as shown. Extend the diagonal lines (as shown by the dashed lines) across the paper. Cut out.

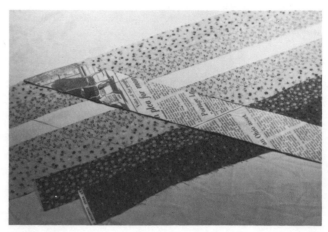

Illus. 96.

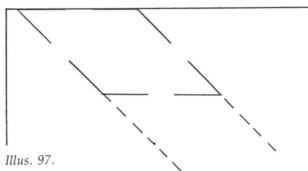

Illus. 97.

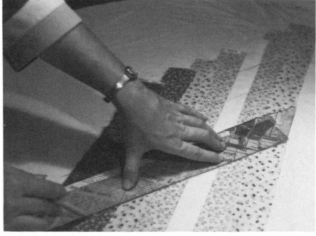

Illus. 98.

11. Spread a completed strip unit in front of you. Lay the paper template at the top edge of strip #1 and adjust the template to fit just inside the beginning of each seam as you go down the fabric. Do not distort the template. If it will not fit just inside the beginning of each seam, move it over a little.

12. Lay a straightedge along one side of the template and draw a line. Repeat on other side.

66

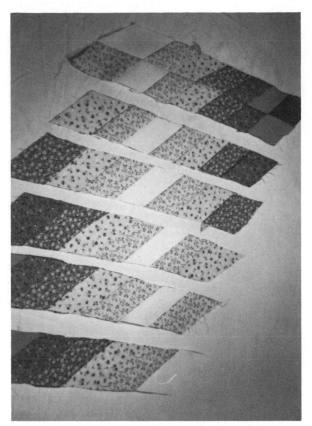

Illus. 99.

Illus. 100.

bias edge will allow a small amount of ease, but do not stretch too much as it will distort the fabric.

14. Press completed diamond thoroughly. Assemble diamond as shown for an eight-point star.

15. Press completed diamond. Lay it out on a flat surface, with paper under the corners and in the triangular spaces. Use a straightedge to draw a pattern for these pieces.

This method can be used for any similar pattern, such as the *Star of Bethlehem*, and also for six-point diamonds arranged in a radiating manner such as the *Lone Star*.

Now place the the template along the second line and draw another line. Continue across fabric until you have drawn eight strips. Cut on the lines.

13. Draw seam allowance on each strip. Pin strips together, in proper sequence, matching diamonds at seam line. They will not match at outer edges, only at seams. Stitch seams. The

Strip-Piecing a Two-Color Diamond

There are a number of patterns that split the diamond in half lengthwise into two colors. *Silver and Gold* and *Star of LeMoyne* are two of these patterns.

There is also a group of four-patch designs, such as *Blazing Star* and *Job's Troubles*, which can be treated in the same way using the method described.

Eight-Point Star

1. Draw templates for the diamond shape.
2. Divide the template in half lengthwise. Measure from the line to the edge of the template to determine the width of the strips needed.
3. Cut two strips, light and dark, to the width determined in Step 2, adding seam allowance.
4. Lay the marked template with the line along the seam line of the fabric strips. Trace around the template and cut out.

There's your whole diamond ready to sew together.

Blazing Star

Traditional piecing instructions for this pattern would allow you to use the same method as for *Job's Troubles*. Sew together the strips for #1 and #2, cut out template shapes, and then set the corner points with the white #3 and add the center piece.

However, this sewing method creates difficulties when you add the second center point. If you change the order of piecing, this design can be sewn with all straight seams.

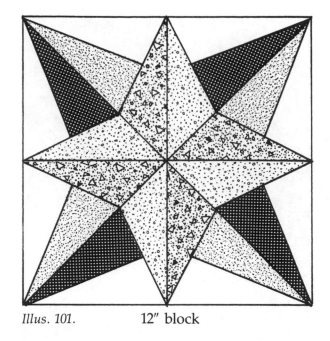

Illus. 101.   12″ block

Join #1 to #3; add #2. Repeat for second side, reversing patterns. Join these two sections diagonally to form a square. Repeat for other three corners; then join the squares.

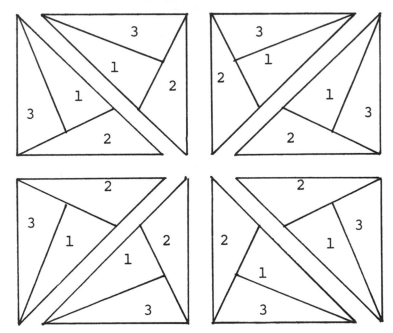

Illus. 102. Assembly.

68

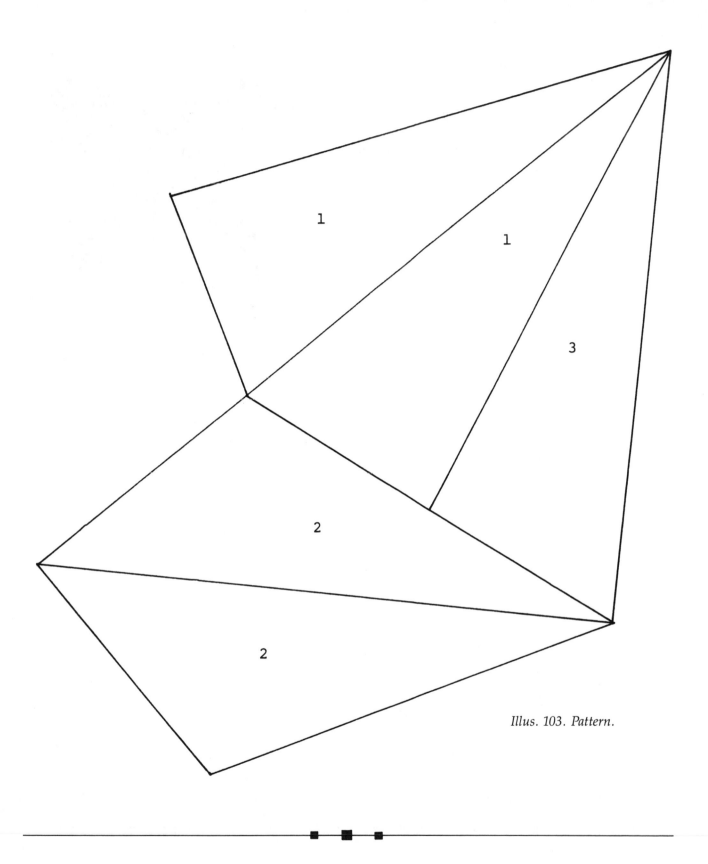

Illus. 103. Pattern.

Job's Troubles

1. Make templates of the patterns given.
2. Cut two strips, light and dark fabric, 4" wide. Seam together.
3. Lay template #1 on the strip lining up the dividing line of the template with the seam line.
4. Cut out.
5. Cut out remaining pattern pieces from template #2. The pattern given is a half-pattern. If you use the pattern as given, adding a seam allowance to all sides, this can be sewn to the completed part #1 in a straight seam, then joined with another like unit in a straight seam to form half the block. If you make a whole pattern out of this piece, you will have to set it in between the points of part #1.

Illus. 104. 12" block.

ADD SEAM ALLOWANCES

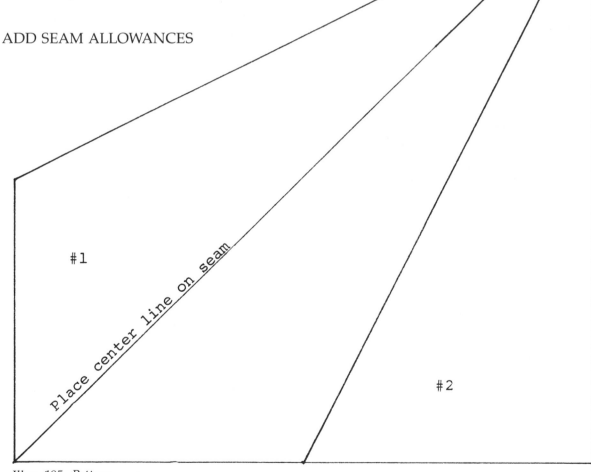

#1

Place center line on seam

#2

Illus. 105. Pattern.

70

ENGLISH-PIECING

This method of piecing is generally used when joining hexagons but also has applications when piecing diamonds. These shapes have a bias edge and the use of the papers helps you handle the pieces without stretching.

1. Add seam allowance to the template and cut out the hexagon shapes from fabric.
2. Make another template without seam allowance and cut out an equal number of paper hexagons. Typing paper is a good weight to use.
3. Lay the paper pattern on the wrong side of the hexagon, turn over the seam allowance and baste.

4. Using a whipstitch, join the hexagons through the fold. Remove the papers.

Grandmother's Flower Garden is a favorite design, which uses hexagons. If piecing this, using very small hexagons, it is better to do it by hand, either sewing the seams together or using the English-piecing method. For larger pieces, since each hexagon is set into the space formed by two other hexagons, the method described above should be used. Whether inserting hexagon or diamond shapes, by sewing only from one end of the seam line to the other you have enough play to smoothly sew in the next shape.

PIECING CURVED SEAMS

Curves in a design probably cause more headaches than any other type of design unit. If you place the adjoining units face up, they fit together beautifully. But turn them over, right sides together, and the curves are going in the wrong direction! One goes out and one goes in!

My first attempt at piecing curves was on the *Drunkard's Path* pattern. I tried endless ways to piece those curves and eventually wound up turning under the seam allowance on the small corner piece and sewing it down with a whipstitch. It worked, but I still wanted to know how to do it on the sewing machine.

I finally achieved success on the *Double Wedding Ring* pattern. The curves are much gentler, which makes them easier to sew. After a little experimentation, I found it was easier to mark the pieces on the right side of the fabric. This way, I can see both seams as I'm trying to match them when sewing. In fact, it is helpful to mark the convex piece on both sides, the right side to match the seam on the concave piece, and the wrong side to provide a seam line to sew along.

First, find the center on both pieces to be joined and mark it, either with a pencil or by ironing a crease at the midpoint. This will help you know that your seam is going to come out even. If you're off at the midpoint, stop, tear it out and start over.

Match the end of the seam on each piece and place it under the needle with the concave or inner curving piece on the bottom, the convex or outward-curving piece on top. Take a couple of stitches to secure the end; then with the needle down in the fabric, lift the top piece and align the two seam lines. Continue stitching for

Illus. 106.

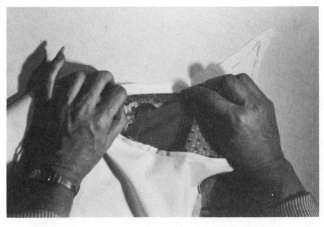

an inch or so, then check again to make sure the seams are meeting properly. Continue stitching and checking until the seam is complete. Clip curves if necessary.

Using this method, you'll wonder why you ever hesitated to sew the *Double Wedding Ring*.

Drunkard's Path and other patterns with a tight curve are a bit more difficult, mainly because the bias edge tends to stretch more when sewing. A pin at each end of the seam line and one at the center point will help control the stretch.

Double Wedding Ring

An all-time favorite pattern is the *Double Wedding Ring*. To piece it accurately requires many, many hours of work due to the large number of small pieces.

You can eliminate many hours of marking, cutting and sewing by strip-piecing the arcs that make up the design. While you won't be able to utilize tiny scrap pieces, lengths of strips from other projects are excellent for this method.

The finished size of the strip can be from 1″ to 2″ wide, depending on your personal preference. The strips used here finish out at 1½″. Add either a ¼″ or ½″ seam allowance and cut out the strips. Seam them together in order desired. The strips need not all be the same length. You can add on as you run out of each strip. Add strips until your constructed fabric is 8½″ wide. Press the seams to one side. Lay template A across the fabric and mark. Add seam allowance and cut out.

Illus. 107.

Illus. 108.

This is a pattern of random scraps and the strips need not all be the same width. They can vary up to an inch.

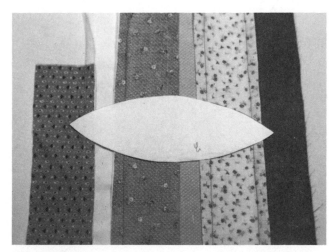

Illus. 109.

Sew the strips together until they measure about 8½″ wide. Lay E crosswise on the strips and mark. Add seam allowance and cut out. Sew these pieces to D as shown in the photo.

With the addition of one more piece to square off the block, the above E and D pieces can be used to create *Reminiscent of the Wedding Ring*.

73

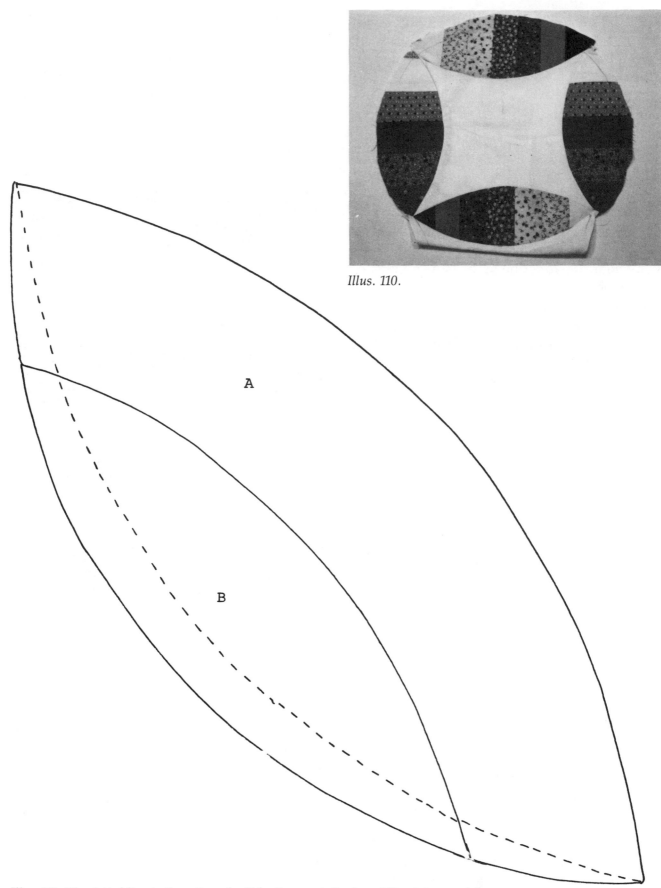

Illus. 110.

A

B

Illus. 111. The dotted line is the pattern for E for Remnant Ovals and Reminiscent of the Wedding Ring.

You could also eliminate F and appliqué the completed circle to a background block.

The rest of the pieces are marked, cut and sewn as usual.

An even easier method is to use an appropriately spaced striped fabric as shown. No seams at all, and once quilted, it looks like the real thing.

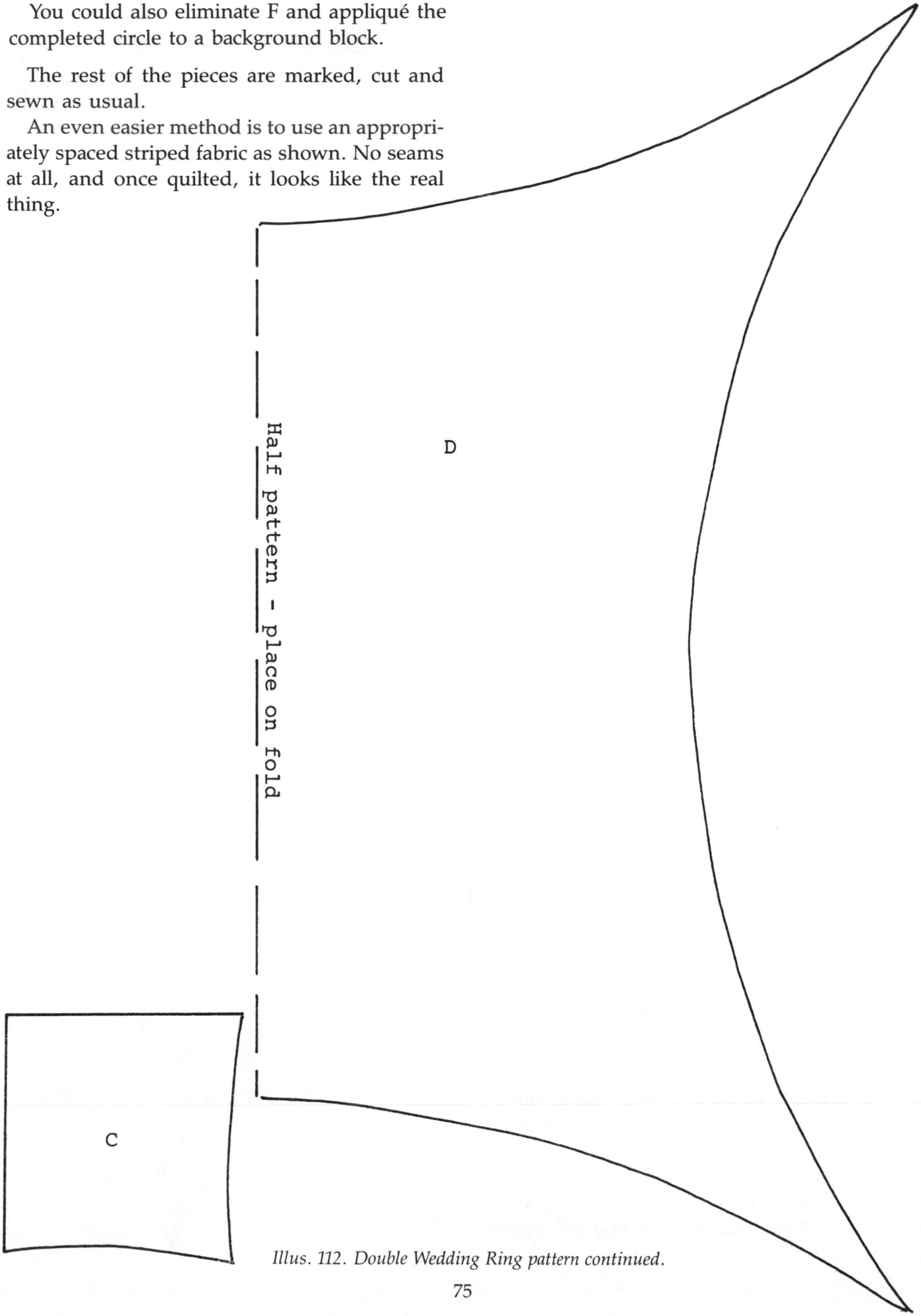

D

Half pattern - place on fold

C

Illus. 112. Double Wedding Ring pattern continued.

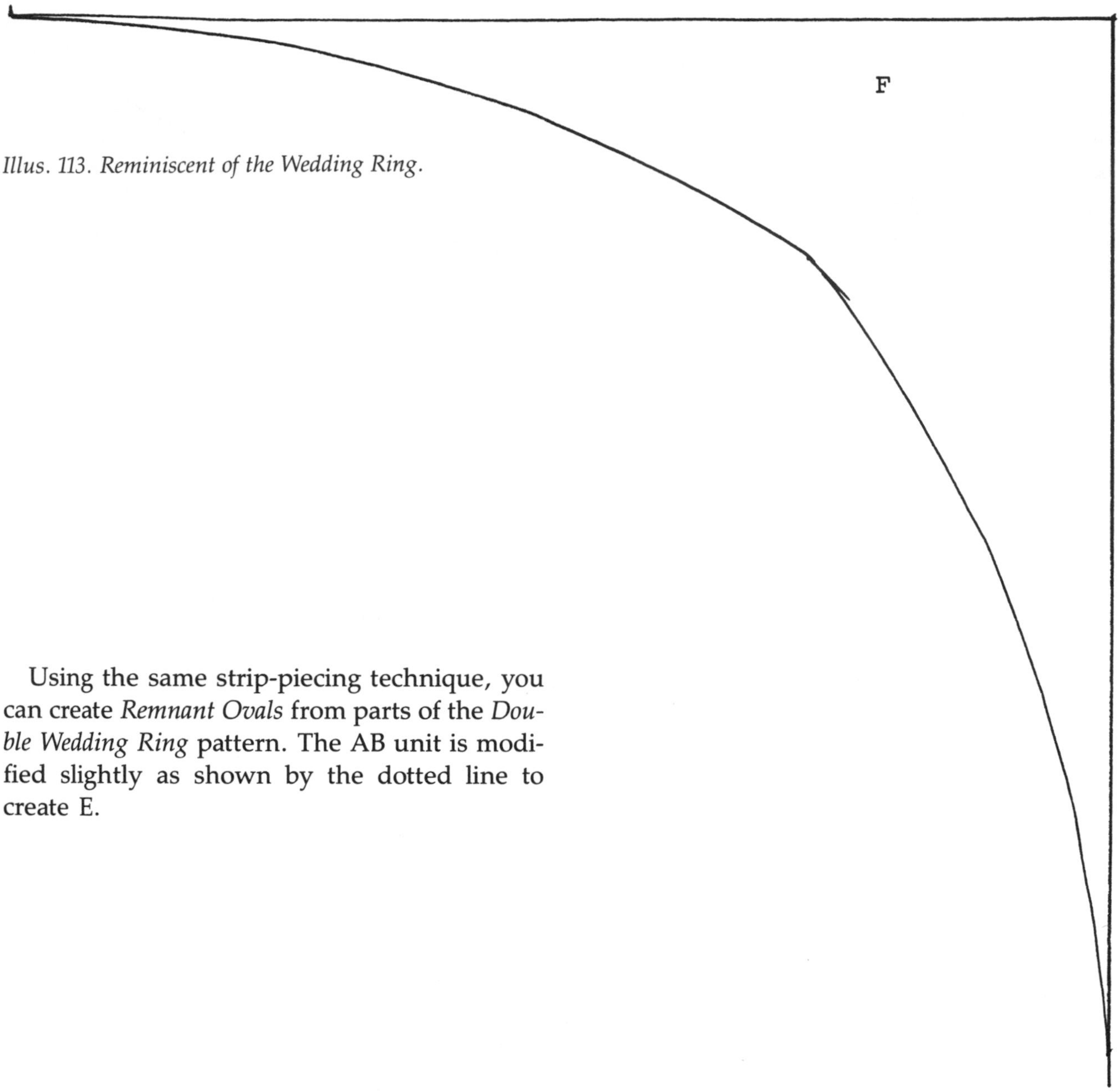

Illus. 113. Reminiscent of the Wedding Ring.

F

Using the same strip-piecing technique, you can create *Remnant Ovals* from parts of the *Double Wedding Ring* pattern. The AB unit is modified slightly as shown by the dotted line to create E.

Cathedral Window

I used to hesitate to make up this pattern because all the little squares are whipstitched together. First, I don't like that much hand-sewing, and second, my hand-sewing leaves a lot to be desired.

My original solution was to zigzag-stitch the squares together, which worked just fine. I still like this method because it leaves a very pretty pattern on the back.

Illus. 114.

76

A new method has come along wherein all parts are sewn by machine. To try this method you will need to cut 11″ squares of white or solid-color fabric.

1. Fold each square in half and sew with a ¼″ seam allowance down the short sides.

2. Bring seams to center, match and pin. Beginning ½″ from center seams, stitch edge to fold. Turn and stitch other side. Turn square right side out.

3. Fold the corners in so that they meet at the center of the square. Press in place.

4. Joining the squares. Open out the fold on two squares. Pin plain side to plain side along fold line. Stitch along fold line. Add more squares in the same manner.

When a square has been added to each side, fold the corners back to the center and tack in place.

5. Cut a 3″ square of print fabric. Place the square over the seam where two folded squares join.

6. Roll the folded edge down over the "window" square. This will form a curve over the print fabric. Blindstitch in place.

After trying this method several times, I find the results less than satisfactory. First, it entails a lot of unnecessary sewing. I can press the folds in place in the traditional way a lot faster than I can sew them.

Secondly, the resulting square is a bias square. If your stitching is off the least little bit, you will not get that square to lie flat. Even if you have sewn it perfectly, it is difficult to press it flat without at least a few wrinkles along the edges.

After some experimentation, I finally settled on the following method:

1. Cut 11″ squares. The number of squares depends on the size of the final coverlet. The beauty of this pattern is that you just keep adding squares until the desired size is reached.

Illus. 115.

2. Fold the square on the diagonal and press to form a guideline.

3. Bring each corner to the center along the pressed lines. Press each fold. Now bring the new corners to the center and press. Follow the previous instructions from 4 through 6.

As I mentioned before, I like the way the zigzag stitch looks along the curved edge. Experiment with all the methods to see which one you like best.

APPLIQUÉ

Appliqué predates traditional piecework by a few hundred years. Ladies of the various courts of Europe showed their skills with the needle by creating lavishly appliquéd clothing and bed coverings. In America, while the majority of quilts made were of the pieced variety, special and masterpiece quilts were invariably appliqué.

Accuracy is important when piecing a quilt, but it is even more so when doing appliqué, since every flaw will show on the surface of the quilt. This may be why so many modern quilters pass up the many lovely appliqué designs.

There are several little tricks that will help you achieve the required accuracy and make appliqué as easy as piecework.

When cutting templates for piecework you have the choice of adding the seam allowance or not, making it a matter of personal preference. For best results when doing appliqué, do not add the seam allowance. This way you have the seam line to follow when turning under the edges.

The second difference is that appliqué pieces should be marked on the right side of the fabric. This eliminates any guesswork as to where the seam line is.

Once you have cut the templates, prepare the background blocks. Press each block; then fold and press it both diagonally and crosswise so that you have eight sections on the block. Using the sections as a guide, lay the templates on the block and trace around each one so that you have an accurate placement guide for each appliqué piece.

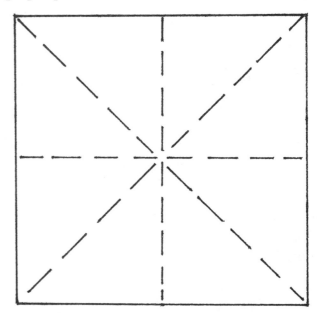

Illus. 116.

Appliqué designs usually contain hundreds of curves, and this is what causes the majority of problems. At this point, your iron is indispensable.

Cut a thin but sturdy template for each piece. (Manila folders are excellent.) Lay the piece

78

wrong side up on the ironing board and lay the lightweight template over it. Start at a fairly straight spot, and bring the seam allowance back over the template until you see the seam line. Press down the seam allowance. Continue around the piece, *clipping curves* as you come to them. By clipping the curves you are able to spread or overlap the seam allowance as needed to prevent folds or puckers on the right side. When all the seam allowance is turned under, remove the template, turn the appliqué right side up, and press again to sharpen the crease.

If the appliqué piece is especially intricate, with lots of curves, you might try running a line of stitching along the seam line; then turn under the seam allowance. The seam allowance almost automatically turns under at this line of stitching.

An alternative method is to use a very lightweight iron-on interfacing to back each appliqué. In this instance, mark the fabric on the wrong side. Trace around the template onto the interfacing and cut the pattern out exactly on the line marked. Press this interfacing within the marked area of the appliqué; then turn under the seam allowance as above. An advantage to the use of the interfacing is that it adds stability to the cut pieces without adding bulk.

When doing machine appliqué, it is not nec-essary to add the seam allowance, since the stitching covers the edge. This is where you will find iron-on interfacing to be really useful. Iron the interfacing onto the wrong side of the fabric before marking or cutting. The interfacing helps prevent stretching of the fabric as you trace around the template.

Some instructions tell you to cut the appliqué with the seam allowance, then trim it off after the zigzag stitching is completed. Accidents can happen when trimming the seam allowance and you also have little threads sticking out from the edges. The interfacing holds the threads in place, thus eliminating any stray pieces sticking out. It also stabilizes bias edges, making the appliqué easier to sew.

Now that all the appliqué pieces are cut, you are ready to place them onto the foundation block. Pinning isn't too satisfactory, especially when doing machine appliqué, since the pins create an ever so slight ripple in the fabrics that will throw the piece off.

Basting is a tried and true method for anchoring the pieces before sewing, but I always have the annoying feeling that I could have completed the sewing in the length of time it took me to baste.

The modern solution is to use a fabric-compatible gluestick. It's quick to apply, there are no wrinkles, and it washes out.

HOW TO MAKE PERFECT CIRCLES

Many patterns, both appliqué and piecework, require a circle for the center of the design. But they are difficult to turn under evenly and smoothly. The following technique makes the job easy.

Mark the seam line on the circle; then cut a lightweight template the exact size of the finished circle. Cut out, adding seam allowance.

Run a basting stitch along the outside edge of the circle, in the seam allowance. This is easier to do by hand, since hand-sewn threads are easier to pull up.

Lay the template on the seam line of the circle; then pull the threads tight around it. This eases all the fullness in evenly. Press. Remove template.

Points

To achieve a nice point, clip off the end of the point seam allowance. Fold the remaining seam allowance down; then fold over the sides of the point.

Illus. 117.

Dresden Plate

Here's a neat little trick you might try the next time you make this version of the *Dresden Plate*.

Use the template, shown on the page, adding seam allowances. Cut out the petals. Fold the petal in half lengthwise and stitch along the seam line across the top. Open out flat and you have perfect turned-under points.

Illus. 118.

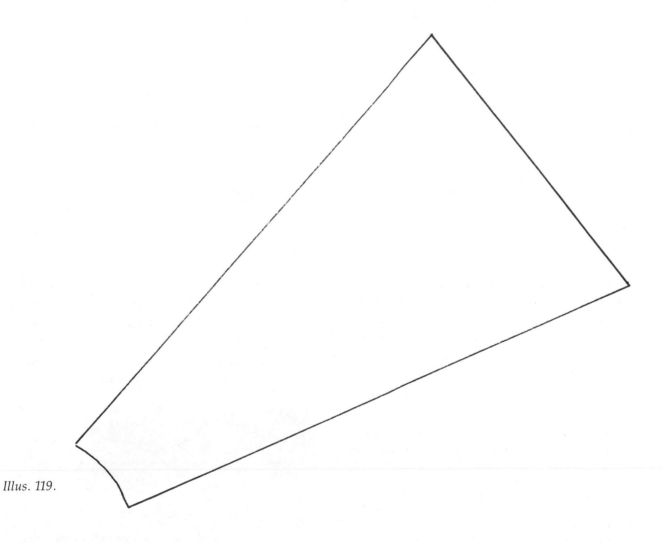

Illus. 119.

THE FINISHING TOUCH

You have a number of options for finishing the edges of your quilt, the simplest being a self-binding. This can be accomplished by either bringing the backing over the edges to the front of the quilt, or taking the quilt top over the backing. To use the quilt top for binding, it is best if there are separate strips of border around the top.

Decide before you begin your quilt how you want to finish it. I'll explain the process by bringing the backing to the front of the quilt, but the process is the same for either. Cut the backing the size of the quilt, plus twice the width of the turnover, plus seam allowance. Bring the batting to the seam allowance of the backing. This way your binding will be stuffed.

Lay the quilt out flat and, beginning at one corner, clip off the tip of the point of the corner. Fold down the seam allowance. Fold over the corner diagonally and lay it on the seam line of the quilt top. Now fold down the sides of the backing to the seam line. You have mitred corners. Stitch in place.

If bringing the top to the back, the additional width must be on the quilt top instead of the backing.

Continuous Bias Binding

This is by far the most common method of binding a quilt. To make the binding, begin with a 36″ square of fabric. If the strips are 2½″ wide, this will yield enough binding for most quilts. If you use wider strips, you will have to make more binding.

1. Cut the fabric in half on the diagonal. Since most fabrics are wider than 36″, let's eliminate cutting it down and just use the full width of the fabric. Press the fabric and straighten the cut edge. Fold the upper left corner over to the right edge of the fabric. Press the fold. Cut the

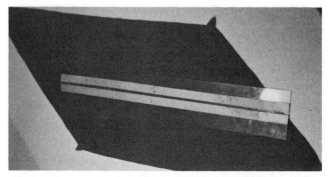

Illus. 120.

fabric along the straight edge at the bottom of the fold. Now cut this in half along the diagonal fold.

2. Sew the two triangles together along the two crosswise straight edges.

3. Mark the seamed bias strip into 2½″ to 3″ wide strips. Make a short cut along the first line.

Illus. 121.

4. Right sides together, bring the upper left corner down to the lower left corner, skipping the cut strip and pinning at the edge of the uncut section. You will have an equal amount of excess on the right side as you have on the left cut side. Stitch the seam.

Illus. 122.

5. Beginning with the cut strip, continue cutting around the bias tube following the lines drawn.

Attaching the Bias Binding

Fold the bias strip in half. Pin the raw edges of the binding to the raw edges of the front of the quilt top. Stitch in place.

Turning the Corner

From each side of the corner, measure the width of the seam allowance and mark. Stitch to this mark, backstitch and break the thread. Bring the binding around the corner, being sure the raw edges are even. Pinch the binding into a fold where it turns the corner. Begin stitching the next side at the point previously marked.

This method might be a little easier and more accurate.

1. Mark each corner the width of the seam allowance as before. Join the marks on the inside edge, forming a small square.

Illus. 123.

2. Stitch to the point marked and break the stitching.

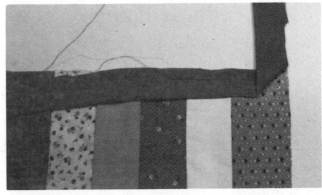

Illus. 124.

3. Fold the binding at a right angle away from the quilt until the binding and quilt form a straight line.

4. Fold the binding down over the fold just made, aligning raw edges of quilt and binding.

Illus. 125.

Begin stitching again at the point on the dot where you broke off. Be sure you don't catch in the fold of the binding. This forms the corner fold.

5. Turn binding to back and stitch in place.

Binding Scalloped Edges

Prepare bias binding and fold in half.

1. Stitch the binding to the front of the quilt, following the edges of the scallops. Do not allow extra binding at the inside points of the scallops.

2. Turn binding to back of quilt. At the inside point of each scallop, form a small fold, which creates a mitred corner at each point. Stitch in place with a slipstitch.

Prairie Points

For a decorative finish to the edge, prairie points adds a nice country touch. Prairie points are made from scrap fabrics cut into squares. The size of the square depends on the size edging you want, but 5" squares are a good place to start. Cut out the squares. You will need quite a few to go around the edge of the quilt.

Fold each square in half diagonally; then fold in half again on the diagonal.

To assemble, lay one triangle in front of you, point up. Fold two layers back even with the point and insert the next triangle, laying it against the folded back edge. Pin in place. Pin

several together; then stitch across the base of the triangle.

Illus. 126.

To attach the strips to the quilt, pull the backing away from the quilt and batting. Pin the strips to the quilt top, right sides together, raw edges even. Sew the strip to the quilt and batting. Open out, placing the seam allowance towards the quilt. Turn under the seam allowance on the backing and blindstitch it in place to the quilt.

Illus. 127.

Ruffles

You can buy ready-made ruffling or go the cheaper route and make your own. Of course, if you make your own, you can make it any color you want to match or contrast with the quilt. Decide whether you want the ruffle around three or four sides of the quilt. Measure the sides you want to place the ruffle on. You will need twice this measurement for the length of the ruffle.

Determine the desired width of the ruffle, double the measurement and add seam allowance. Join the ends, forming a circle. Fold the fabric in half widthwise and run two lines of basting along the raw edges.

Place pins or markers every 24″ to 36″. Remember, the ruffle is twice as long as you need to go around the quilt. The markers will help you to draw the threads evenly around the ruffle and know that it will fit around the quilt.

The ruffle is applied in the same way as prairie points.

QUILTING

Choosing a Quilting Design*

Because fancy quilt designs will not show up against a patterned background, intricate quilting designs are usually used to fill alternate plain blocks and borders or where you have large areas of unpatterned space to fill.

For geometric patterns that are set solid, you have many options when selecting a quilting design.

The simplest choice is outline quilting. Using this method you quilt three-eighths to one-

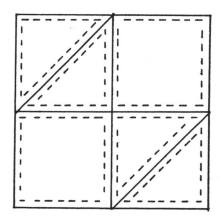

Illus. 128.

*The material that follows on pages 81–86 is adapted from my book *Quilting Techniques and Patterns for Machine Stitching*. New York: Sterling Publishing Co., 1985.

quarter inch on each side of all seam lines. A second method of outline quilting is to quilt "in the ditch," which means directly in the seam line of each piece. You sew only one line of stitching; so the quilting is finished faster than when using the double-line quilting.

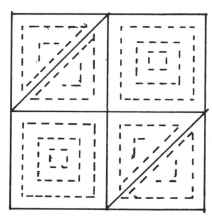

Illus. 129.

If the individual patches of the block are large, leaving more than one to one and a half inches unquilted, you can fill in the pieces with shadow quilting. This consists of repeating the outline quilting in succeeding rows to fill in the area.

In some cases you may want to emphasize the illusion created by the quilt pattern. *Ka-*

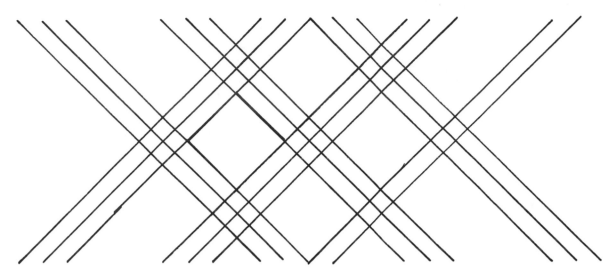

Illus. 130.

leidoscope gives the illusion of large interlocking angular circles when the blocks are joined. To emphasize this design element, quilt around the circles, ignoring the seam lines, then shadow-quilt to the center.

will have a pattern of diamonds. Although most people seem to find the diamond design more visually exciting, you can also run the lines straight up and down and crosswise to form squares. You might also try multiple lines to form an interesting design as shown in Illus. 131.

A general rule of thumb is to use straight-line quilting with circular patterns and circular designs with geometric patterns. The geometric design in Illus. 132 shows one of the many possibilities for using circles to enhance a quilt.

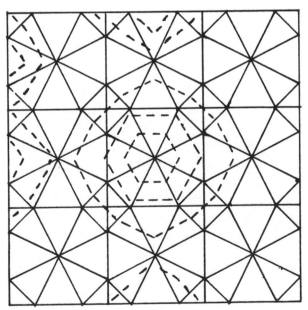

Illus. 131.

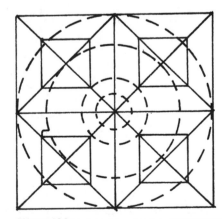

Illus. 132.

Or you can ignore the pattern of the top entirely and use an overall design. The most common design for this purpose is the use of diagonal lines spaced one-half to one inch apart across the quilt top. If you run another line of diagonal lines in the opposite direction, you

Templates for circles can be anything from a cup to a pan lid depending on the size of circle you need. Of course, there's always a compass to fall back on. The clamshell is one of the most

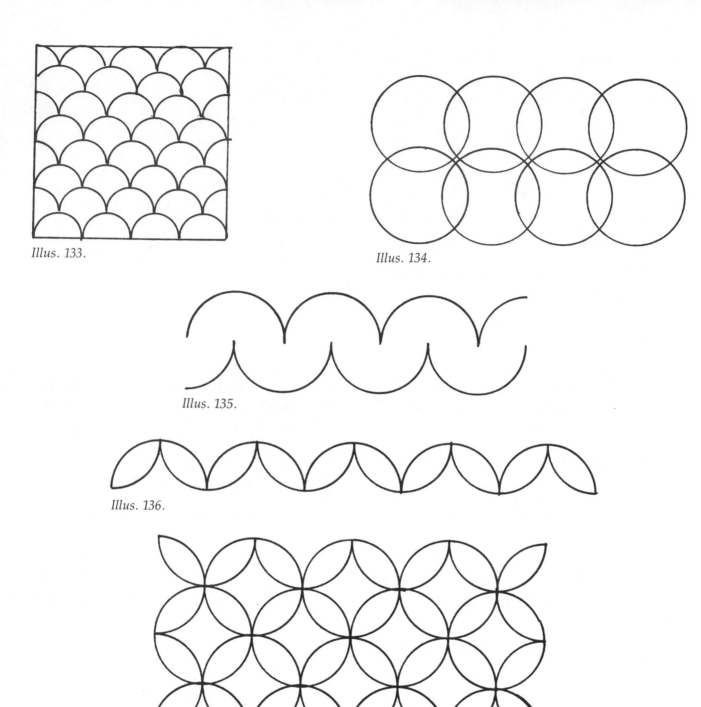

Illus. 133.

Illus. 134.

Illus. 135.

Illus. 136.

Illus. 137.

popular circle designs, but there are many other possibilities. Experiment with different arrangements and sizes until you come up with a pleasing design. Illus. 133–137 provide some ideas to get you started.

You can also create some interesting designs by using hexagons and pentagons.

Many quilt patterns consist of a pieced half set with a solid plain half as in the *Sawtooth* pattern. The plain half can be quilted using an elaborate motif, and outline quilting can be used for the pieced half, or you could repeat the pieced design on the plain half. This idea will work beautifully on an appliqué quilt set with alternate plain blocks, especially if stuffed quilting is used on the plain blocks to emphasize the design. (See Illus. 138.)

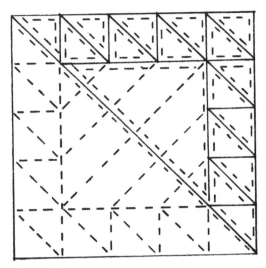

Illus. 138.

Transferring the Design

At present, quilting is enjoying such popularity that new shops are springing up all across the country which cater to the demand for quilting supplies. Sturdy plastic stencils are available in these shops, and selections range from a few standard feather designs in some to hundreds of different design stencils in others.

Manufacturers are constantly bringing out new items to make the job easier. One manufacturer has recently marketed a quilting stencil that you stick to the fabric; you then quilt around the outline of the design, after which you move the stencil to the next block. No marking is needed.

However, in the future, as in the past, these tools may not be so easy to come by. You also have greater flexibility in your choice of design if you are not confined to ready-made stencils. And it's cheaper to make your own.

If your quilting design is a straight-line, all-over pattern, you need nothing more elaborate than a ruler and a pencil to mark directly on the

fabric. But if you are using a more elaborate design, the marking process becomes a two-step operation. First you must make a working pattern, either a stencil or a perforated pattern sheet. The second step is the actual marking of the fabric.

Making the Pattern Sheet

Stencils.* The preferred material for a stencil is a sheet of clear, heavy plastic that is soft enough to cut. Lightweight plastic sheets can be used, but the edges tend to move around when you trace the design onto the fabric. Colored plastic sheets can also be used, but you will have to transfer the design to the plastic before you cut it out.

You will need a sharp craft knife or a double-bladed knife. This type of knife has two blades side by side so that you can cut both sides of the line with one cut. It can be adjusted to varying widths by simply maintaining pressure on the hand grip. Be sure to have extra blades on hand so that you can change them when they start to get dull. Dull blades make the work harder and the lines are not as cleanly cut.

You will also need a sheet of glass large enough to cover the pattern.

Tape your design pattern to the underside of the glass, face up. Tape your clear plastic sheet on top of the glass so you can see your design through it.

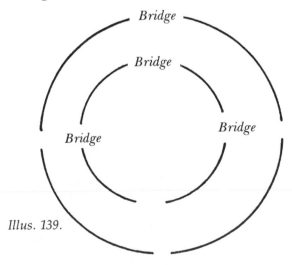

Illus. 139.

*For elaborate designs that will be repeated several times on the quilt top, a stencil is the fastest and easiest method to use.

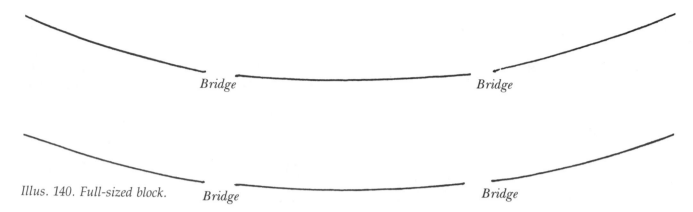

Illus. 140. Full-sized block.

Bridge Bridge

Bridge Bridge

Study your design so you can decide where to leave "bridges." These are small areas of un-cut plastic that will hold the stencil together. When you start quilting, you ignore the broken line and quilt directly over the bridge.

The best example for the need of a bridge is if you are cutting a series of circles. If a bridge is not left, all the circles will fall out, leaving only the largest one.

Whenever two lines cross, a bridge should be left to stabilize the pattern so that it won't move around when you are tracing it. Long curves should have bridges spaced evenly along the line of the curve, again to prevent movement of the pattern while tracing.

Use a soft-tip marker to place a little line on

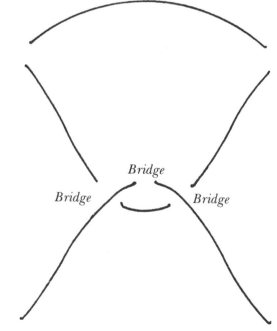

Bridge

Bridge Bridge

Illus. 141.

the areas where you will leave a bridge. With your knife, cut along the line of the pattern be-tween two bridges. Go back and cut the other side of the line and each end. The cut line should be about one-sixteenth of an inch wide, just wide enough for the point of a pencil to move along easily. If using a double-bladed knife, adjust the width to one-sixteenth inch and cut along the line, cutting both sides at once. When you reach the end, cut crosswise. Measure over one-eighth inch to allow for the bridge, and continue cutting the line to the next bridge.

A sheet of hard cardboard can be used for a stencil as well as the colored plastic I mentioned before. When using cardboard, use a manila folder or something similar. The cardboard used for tablet backs is not suitable because it is very soft and breaks down quickly from the action of the pencil against the edges. If using cardboard or colored plastic, your first step is to transfer the design to the cardboard. You then proceed in the same manner as with a plastic stencil.

Perforated Patterns

This type of pattern was quite common during the thirties and even earlier. It is not as perma-nent as a stencil because the paper is subject to wear and tear and it is a bit messy to use since you use chalk to transfer the design to the fab-ric, but it is quicker and easier to make than a stencil.

Trace the selected design onto a sheet of pa-per. Place the largest needle possible in your sewing machine; then sew over the lines of the design with an unthreaded needle. The design is transferred to the fabric by placing the pattern sheet on the quilt top and pouncing tailor's chalk through the holes with either a powder puff or cotton ball.

If the design consists of long, easy curves, you could use a toothed tracing wheel to punch holes in the pattern. This results in larger holes, making it easier to pounce the chalk through.

Mark small sections at a time, since the chalk tends to rub off during the quilting process.

Once your pattern is completed, you are ready for the actual transfer to the fabric. Easy removal of the lines on the quilt top is your major consideration when choosing a method to use for transferring the design. For those of you who don't like to wash your quilts in the washing machine, it is doubly important that you choose a method of marking that will brush off easily.

The simplest method is to use a hard lead pencil—at least a #3 lead. Soft lead leaves a darker line, but tends to smudge, leaving dirty marks on the quilt. The pencil is used with stencils, and as mentioned before, you can work directly on the top for straight-line quilting, using a ruler and pencil.

Another tool for marking straight lines is carpenter's or tailor's chalk. A carpenter's chalk line is the easiest to use, since the line is attached to a container which holds the chalk. You merely wind the line into the container to coat it with chalk; then pull it out to use. You will also need someone to help you.

Spread the quilt top out flat, either on a large table or on the floor. Position your helper on one side of the quilt while you are on the other side. Stretch the chalked line tightly across the quilt, just barely touching the surface. Lift the center of the line and snap it quickly.

Occasionally, you may want to use a design only once. Lay the fabric directly over the pattern and trace it through the fabric with a pencil. However, if the fabric is too heavy to see through, or colored, you can't do this. An alternative is to use dressmaker's carbon paper.

Trace the design onto a sheet of paper to make a working pattern. Position the working pattern on the block; then slip a piece of dressmaker's carbon under the pattern and trace over the design with a pencil. For a very simple design you could use a toothed tracing wheel. The tracing wheel will leave small dots rather than a solid line. The major drawback in using this method is that it may take two or three washings for the lines to come out, especially the colored carbons.

Another alternative to a stencil is the use of a transfer pencil. The transfer pencil makes an iron-on sheet that can be reused several times. It's very easy to make and it makes transferring the design a breeze. Like the dressmaker's carbon, though, it may take two or three washings for the marks to come out of the fabric.

To make the transfer sheet you need only a sheet of paper and a transfer pencil. Lay the paper over the design to be transferred and trace it as you would with a regular pencil. The transfer pencil dulls quickly; so keep a pencil sharpener handy so that you can maintain a fine line.

Lay the finished drawing face down on your block and press with a warm iron. I usually set it on "wool."

One other method you may want to try when quilting straight lines is the use of masking tape. With this method, you have no lines at all to remove when the quilting is finished.

Determine how far apart you want the lines to be; then buy masking tape of an appropriate width. Tear off a suitable length and press it onto the fabric in the design you have chosen. Quilt along both sides of the tape. Remove the tape and stretch a new length for your next line of quilting.

Sources for Design Ideas

No matter how many quilting designs you have available to you, the day will come when none of them quite fits the bill for the quilt you are working on. This is the time to start experimenting on your own.

Look at everyday objects in outline form, eliminating the details. This is the basis of a quilting design. When leafing through magazines look at the outline of the design; then add details as needed to suit the purpose of quilting.

Your first source of design ideas an be found among your quilting patterns. Many appliqué patterns transform beautifully into quilting designs. How about a snowflake or floral motif or the sunbonnet patterns for a child's quilt?

Examine your embroidery patterns. If you eliminate some of the details, many of them translate into quilt designs. The same is true of patterns that are intended for tole and decorative painting. And don't forget those stencil-painting patterns.

I used to recommend coloring books for simple children's designs, but after looking through some on the newsstand, I couldn't find any with simple toys and animals in outline form. If you can find some, they make great designs. You may have to add a few details to meet the requirements of quilting. As an alternative, look for pictures that you can simplify for quilting.

Many patterns designed for other crafts can be made into quilting designs. I recently saw a basket pattern designed for cut-paper silhouettes that would make a beautiful quilting design. One of my designs was taken directly from the wallpaper in my bathroom.

When all else fails you can always fall back on folded paper cutouts. Cut a sheet of paper the size of the desired block design; then fold it two, three or four times, lengthwise, crosswise, on the diagonal. Now cut the designs along the folds. Open it out to see what you have created. If you don't like it, try again.

Hand-Quilting

For hand-quilting you will need a frame. If you have the space, use a full-sized frame, which allows you to stretch the whole quilt before you begin sewing. If space is a problem, a quilting hoop will serve equally well, although you have to keep moving the hoop as you complete each section.

To prepare the quilt for mounting, you must first assemble the three layers of the quilt: the backing, the filler or batt, and the top. Spread the backing out flat on the floor; then spread the batt over the backing, stretching slightly to fit, if necessary. If more than slight stretching is required, don't; instead add more batting. Now lay the pressed top on the batt and smooth it out. Baste the three layers together diagonally, horizontally and vertically. The quilt is now ready to mount.

With the quilt stretched out on the floor, lay one of the muslin-covered bars of the frame at the top of the quilt and the other bar at the bottom. Using heavy thread, baste the quilt to the bars, making sure it is secured tightly enough to withstand the stretching action of the frame.

Roll the quilt tightly onto one bar, leaving enough free to stretch across the frame. Replace the bars in the frame, adjusting the quilt so that it is stretched tautly in the frame.

If using a hoop, follow the same procedure for basting. Place the quilt in the hoop, starting in the center and working towards the edges. Quilt this center section; then move the hoop outward for the next section. When that section is complete, move the hoop to the other side of the center section so that the top is worked evenly from the center to the edges. When you reach the edges you may have to dispense with the hoop and quilt the remainder in your lap.

I'd like to add a little note here. I've found it easier to quilt with the hoop if the quilt is put on backwards; that is, the larger piece to the back of the quilt and the smaller one on top, so that the surface being worked on is recessed. The fabric is held taut, but there is a little more play which makes it easier to take smaller stitches. At least it does for me.

If you have difficulty making small stitches using a hoop or a frame, try quilting without them. Since the fabric isn't pulled tight, you can manipulate it so that smaller stitches are possible. Just be sure that you don't pull the threads too tight, which will cause puckers. Work small sections at a time; then smooth it out to make sure it lies flat.

Some patterns, such as *Lone Star* or *Circular* designs have a tendency to cup in the center, so this method shouldn't be used to quilt these patterns. They need the stretching, so that the finished quilt will lie flat.

Machine-Quilting

I am a firm believer in machine-quilting. In fact, my hand-quilting is so bad and takes so long, that I've given it up entirely and do all my quilting on the machine. And contrary to popular opinion, any design can be machine-quilted.

If you have ever done machine embroidery, you'll have no problems with machine-quilting, and even if you haven't it won't take long to get the knack of manipulating the quilt under the needle.

First, a word of warning. If you are planning to enter your quilts in competition, check the rules before you machine-quilt. Many shows insist that the quilting be done by hand.

You are also going to discover that my methods differ drastically from those of other writers, but do try them before you decide that this is not the proper way to do things.

My main divergence from the "norm" is that I do not baste the three layers together before sewing. The outstanding characteristic of fabric is that it does stretch, so rather than trying to bludgeon it into submission with extensive basting, I make allowances for this characteristic.

Step one is to loosen the pressure on the presser foot. Either set the machine for darn or remove the pressure altogether. Some instructions I've read say that after you have basted thoroughly, tighten the pressure on the presser foot. However, this causes the foot to grab the fabric, creating puckers that pile up on the basting lines. Even normal pressure will cause the stitches to pile up on the basting lines.

Since I am not going to baste the layers together, my second step must be to assume that I will have some shifting of the fabric. To make allowance for this, I cut the backing fabric one or two inches larger all around, depending on whether I am quilting the whole top or by the block. A bit more shifting can be expected if you are quilting the whole top. Lay the backing out on the floor and smooth it out. Spread the batting over the backing, making sure it reaches the edges. Now spread the top over the batting and pin it with straight pins here and there. I've actually found very little slippage in the three layers since the cloth seems to stick to the batting.

If you are quilting the whole top as a unit, it is easier if you use outline quilting or straight-line quilting. The quilt is quite heavy and not very maneuverable. A large table on which to sew is an absolute must. It helps keep the quilt flat, thus cutting down on any shifting. Position your machine at one end of the table so you can spread the quilt out and support its weight.

Slide the edge of the quilt under the presser foot and roll it up to the center. The center section is the most difficult because so much fabric is rolled under the machine. As you move out towards the edges it gets easier. Following the seam line from the center, stitch to the outer edge of the quilt, smoothing out the fabric as you go. Stitch two or three rows in this direction; then turn the quilt and stitch two or three rows in the opposite direction. Check frequently to make sure that the backing fabric is still smooth. This alternating technique helps keep the quilt smooth and flat.

If your top is of simple design that requires only straight-line stitching, you can start at one end of the quilt and work to the other end. In this case, the backing fabric should be longer on the end and sides towards which you are sewing so that any shift in the fabric is covered by the backing when finished. Always start sewing from the same end.

If you are quilting an intricate design it is easier to quilt by the block or in sections of four or six blocks. You can also do it in strips of blocks.

When quilting by the block or in small sections, there will be less shifting of the fabric so that the backing can be cut only one inch larger all around than the block or strips. Cut the batting the size of the quilt top section or block. Quilt in the design, being sure not to quilt beyond the seam line into the seam allowance.

To assemble the quilted blocks, trim the backing even with the quilt block. Lay the quilted blocks right sides together, matching seams, and pin, being sure to fold the backing out of the way so that it doesn't catch in the seam line. Stitch the blocks together, adding blocks in the same manner to complete the first row. Before adding the next row or section I've found it easier to finish the seams on the back. Turn the quilt over and smooth it out. Smooth one edge of the backing over the seam line, and under the other edge, being sure that the quilt top remains flat. Fold under the seam allowance on the other edge and lay it over the first edge. Stitch in place with a slipstitch. Now go back and finish the quilting across the seams. The seams on the back will fade into the quilting.

If you have quilted by the block and dislike the seams on the back, a nice finish is to lay lattice strips over the seams. This forms a frame around each block on the back of the quilt.

There is another method of quilting that you might like to try if you're really in a hurry. In this method, the piecing and quilting are done at the same time. The only objection I have to the method is that the quilting does not appear on the top of the quilt.

Diagonal designs or any designs without cross-seams can be adapted to this method. One thing to keep in mind is that the pattern pieces must be within the 2″ to 4″ size recommended for spacing of quilting lines. This will probably mean that the block size will have to be reduced.

For illustration I've selected *Birds in the Air*, a diagonal design with no cross-seams. I've scaled it to a 4″ block, since the outer limit for quilting lines is 4″.

Birds in the Air

1. Cut backing blocks 5″ square.
2. Cut batting 4″ square.
3. Cut out pattern pieces.
4. Follow the diagram shown for order of sewing the pieces in place.

Illus. 142.

Position 1 at the corner and lay 2 over it, wrong sides together. Stitch. Lay 3 over the square wrong sides together and stitch. Continue until all pieces are sewn.

You may find it helpful to draw in the seam allowance on the backing block.

All stitching should begin and end at the seam line, leaving the seam allowance free for joining the blocks.

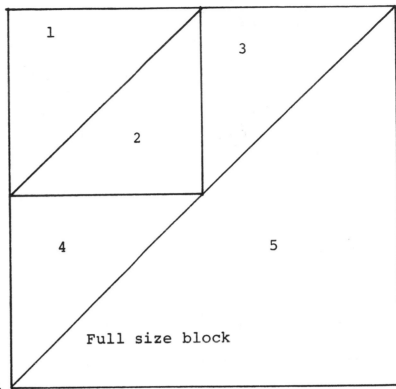

Illus. 143. Full-sized block.

To join the blocks, place two blocks together, right sides facing. Lay back the seam allowance on the backing square and stitch the two pieced squares together. Continue adding squares until you reach the desired width of the row. Make a second row, and add to the first row in the same manner.

To finish the back, turn under the seam allowance on one side, and bring the other seam allowance under this one. Slipstitch.

There are a number of patterns that at first glance don't appear to be adaptable to this method, but if you break them down you will see that they are made up of four blocks that are exactly the same. In this case, you would work each square of the block, then join them together as you would join any other blocks.

A few examples are on the following page.

Southern Belle

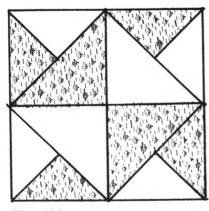

Illus. 144.

Each unit = 4″ for block size of 8″.
Make four and join to form the block.

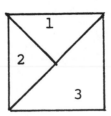

Illus. 145.

Crossed Canoes

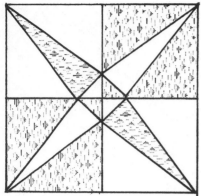

Illus. 146.

Each unit = 4″ for an 8″ block.
Make four as illustrated and join.

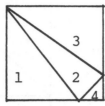

Illus. 147.

Mrs. Taft's Choice

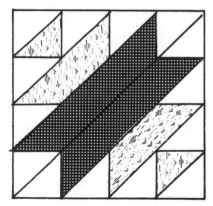

Illus. 148.

12″ block, each square = 1½″.
You could go to a 16″ block, making each square equal 2″.
Make two as shown and join in a diagonal seam across the center.

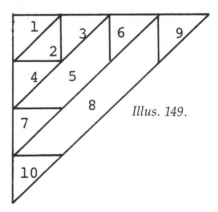

Illus. 149.

APPENDICES

A TREASURY OF SHORTCUT PATCHWORK PATTERNS

The following patchwork patterns are all classic and popular patterns; most of which have appeared in previous books of mine. All of them are adaptable to the shortcut methods that are shown in this book.

Bear's Paw

BLOCK SIZE: 14″
QUILT SIZE: 84″ × 84″
NO. OF BLOCKS: 36

PIECES PER BLOCK			PER QUILT
A	4	Print	144
B	4	Print	144
	1	Plain	36
C	16	Print	576
	16	Plain	576
D	4	Plain	144

FABRIC REQUIRED
4¾ yards Plain
¼ yard scrap fabric per block or a total of 6 yards

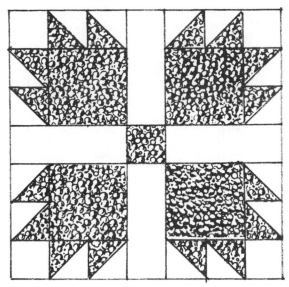

Illus. 150.

A

ADD SEAM ALLOWANCES

Illus. 151.

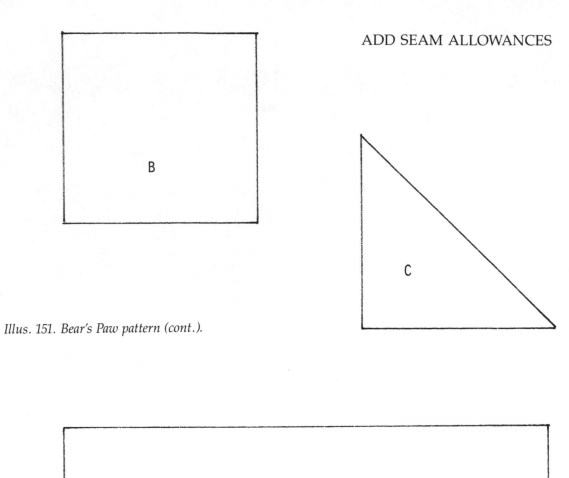

Illus. 151. Bear's Paw pattern (cont.).

Bird's Nest

BLOCK SIZE: 15″
QUILT SIZE: 74″ × 90″
NO. OF BLOCKS: 30

PIECES PER BLOCK		PER QUILT
A	4 Dark	120
B	4 Dark	120
	12 White	360
C	12 White	360
D	9 Print	270
E	12 White	360

FABRIC REQUIRED
6½ yards White
1½ yards Blue Print
4 yards Dark Green

Illus. 152.

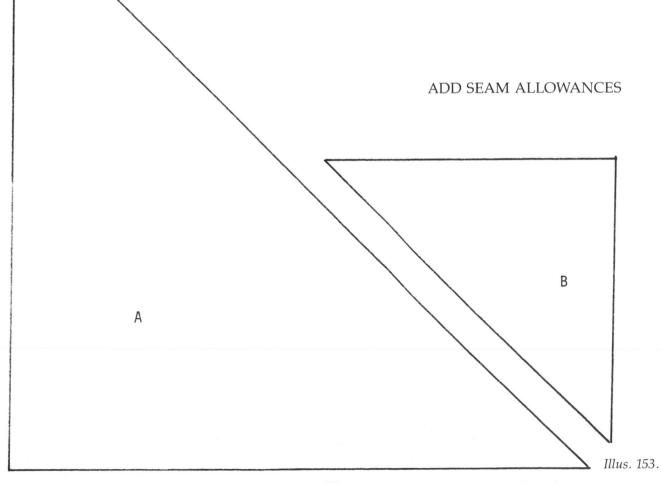

ADD SEAM ALLOWANCES

A

B

Illus. 153.

103

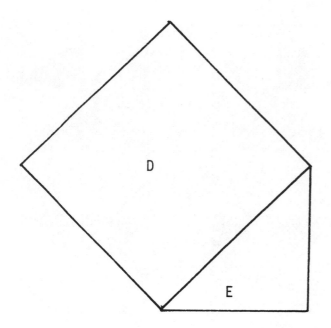

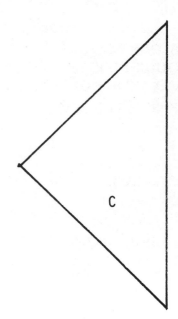

ADD SEAM ALLOWANCES

Illus. 153. Bird's Nest pattern (cont.).

Bow Tie

BLOCK SIZE: 8″
QUILT SIZE: 80″ × 88″
NO. OF BLOCKS: 110

PIECES PER BLOCK	PER QUILT
A 2 White	220
2 Print Scrap	220
B 1 Dark Scrap	110

FABRIC REQUIRED

3½ yards White
5″ × 9″ scrap per block
3″ × 3″ Dark Scrap per block

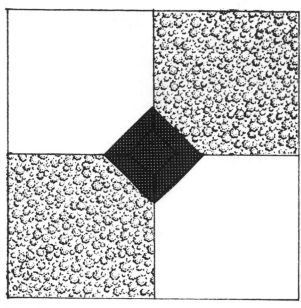

Illus. 154.

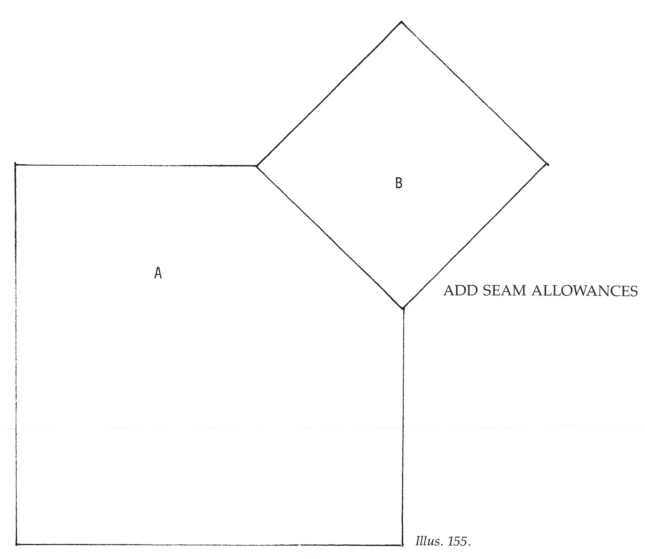

ADD SEAM ALLOWANCES

Illus. 155.

Card Tricks

BLOCK SIZE: 12″
QUILT SIZE: 84″ × 84″
NO. OF BLOCKS: 49

PIECES PER BLOCK		PER QUILT
A	4 White	196
	4 Print	196
	4 Plain	196
B	4 White	196
	4 Print	196
	4 Plain	196

FABRIC REQUIRED

4 yards White

This is usually made as a scrap quilt with different coordinating scraps for each block.

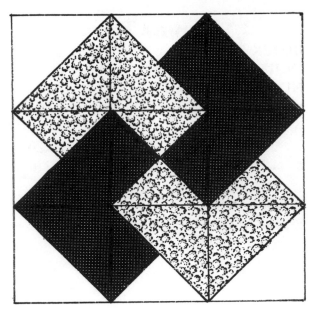

Illus. 156.

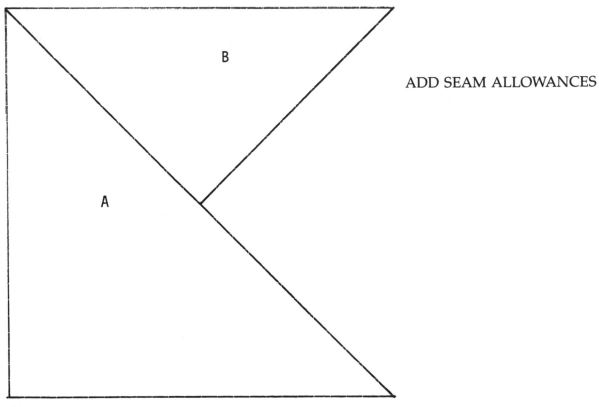

ADD SEAM ALLOWANCES

Illus. 157.

Clay's Choice

BLOCK SIZE: 12″
QUILT SIZE: 84″ × 96″
NO. OF BLOCKS: 56

PIECES PER BLOCK		PER QUILT
A	4 Print	224
	4 White	224
B	8 Dark	448
	4 White	224
	4 Print	224

FABRIC REQUIRED
4 yards Print
3½ yards Dark
4 yards White

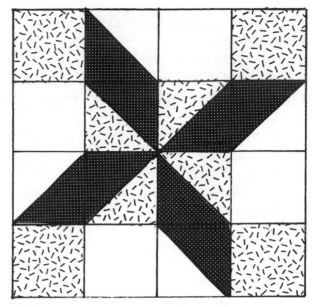

Illus. 158.

I have eliminated a separate pattern for the dark center pieces. These are assembled from half-square triangles, which, if you use the method presented in this book, you will find is much quicker even though you are dealing with more pieces. It also uses slightly less fabric.

ADD SEAM ALLOWANCES

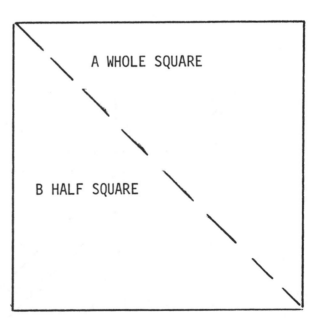

A WHOLE SQUARE

B HALF SQUARE

Illus. 159.

Crazy Ann

BLOCK SIZE: 10″
QUILT SIZE: 80″ × 80″
NO. OF BLOCKS: 64

PIECES PER BLOCK		PER QUILT
A	5 Dark	320
B	8 White	512
C	4 Print	256
D	4 Dark	256
	4 White	256

FABRIC REQUIRED
3¾ yards Dark
5 yards White
3 yards Print

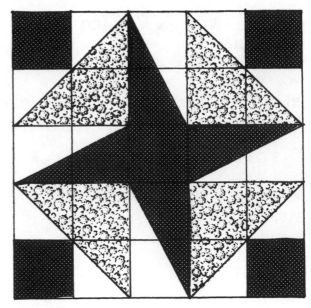

Illus. 160.

ADD SEAM ALLOWANCES

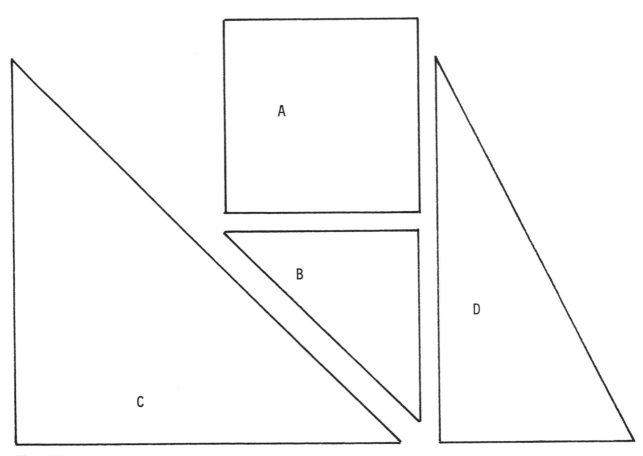

Illus. 161.

Double Pinwheel

BLOCK SIZE: 10″
QUILT SIZE: 80″ × 80″
NO. OF BLOCKS: 64

PIECES PER BLOCK	PER QUILT
A 4 Print	256
B 4 Dark	256
4 Plain	256

FABRIC REQUIRED

4⅔ yards Print
1⅔ yards Dark
1⅔ yards Plain

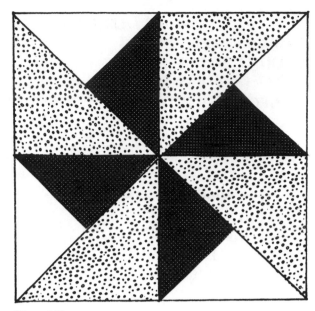

Illus. 162.

ADD SEAM ALLOWANCES

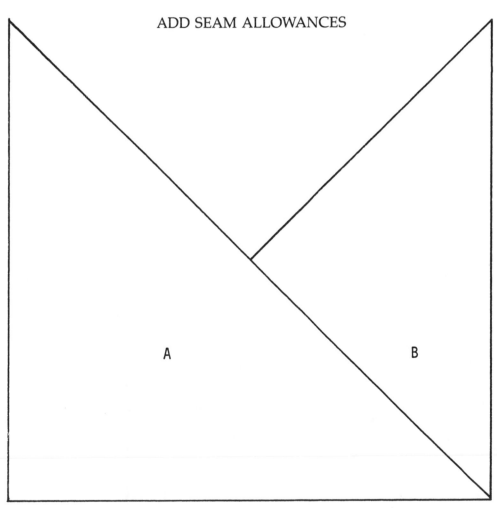

A   B

Illus. 163.

54-40 or Fight

BLOCK SIZE: 12"
QUILT SIZE: 84" × 96"
NO. OF BLOCKS: 56

PIECES PER BLOCK		PER QUILT
A	2 Dark	112
	10 White	560
	8 Print	448
B	8 Dark	448
C	4 White	224

FABRIC REQUIRED
4½ yards Dark
2½ yards Print
5½ yards White

Illus. 164.

ADD SEAM ALLOWANCES

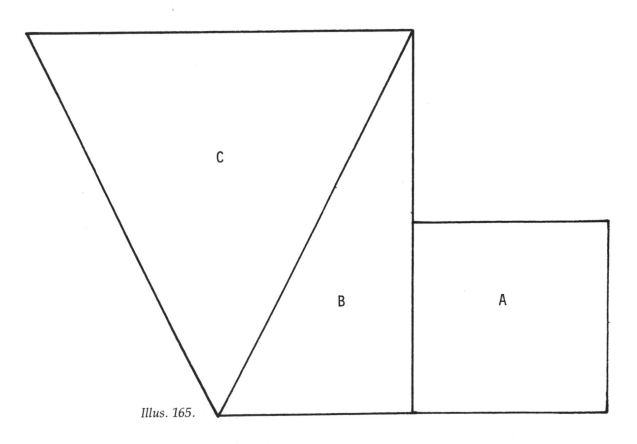

C

B

A

Illus. 165.

110

Grape Basket

BLOCK SIZE: 10"
QUILT SIZE: 84" × 84"
NO. OF BLOCKS: 36 Pieced
                       25 Plain

PIECES PER BLOCK			PER QUILT
A	1	Plain	36
B	11	Print Scrap	396
	7	Plain	252
C	2	Plain	72
D	2	Dark	72
E	2	Plain	72
F	2	Plain	72
	25	11" squares, Plain	
	20	half-squares, Plain	
	4	quarter-squares, Plain	

FABRIC REQUIRED
9¾ yards Plain or White
⅛ yard Assorted scraps
1 yard Dark

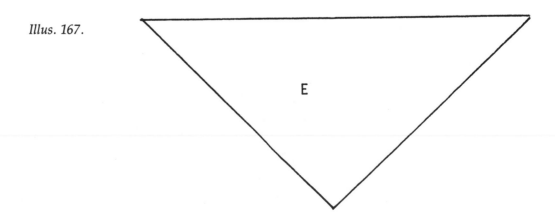

Illus. 166.

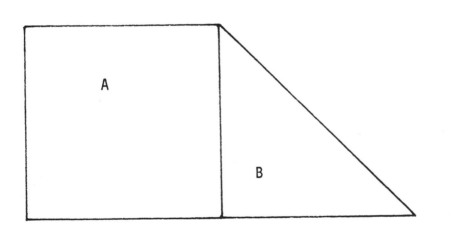

ADD SEAM ALLOWANCES

Illus. 167.

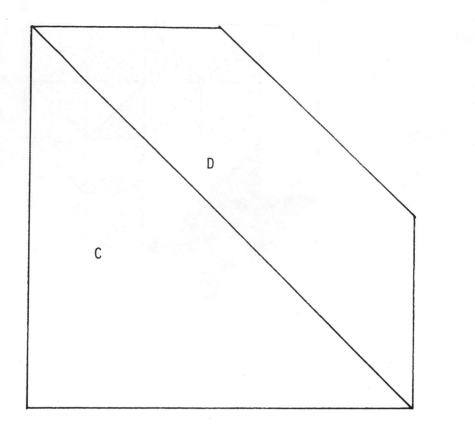

Illus. 167. Grape Basket pattern (cont.).

ADD SEAM ALLOWANCES

Guiding Star

BLOCK SIZE: 12″
QUILT SIZE: 72″ × 84″
NO. OF BLOCKS: 42

PIECES PER BLOCK		PER QUILT
A	8 White	336
B	4 Dark	168
C	4 White	168
D	8 Dark	336

FABRIC REQUIRED
6 yards White
6½ yards Dark

Illus. 168.

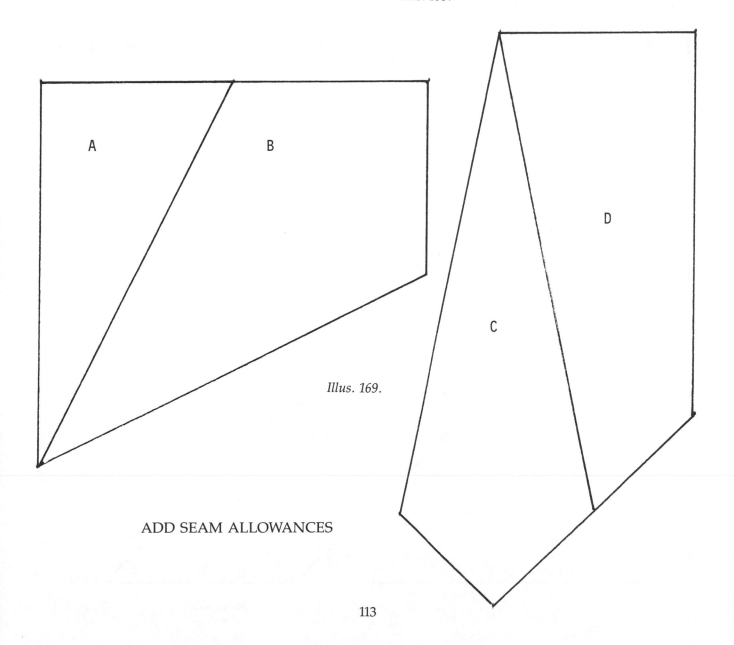

Illus. 169.

ADD SEAM ALLOWANCES

Handy Andy

BLOCK SIZE: 10″
QUILT SIZE: 80″ × 90″
NO. OF BLOCKS: 72

PIECES PER BLOCK			PER QUILT
A	5	Plain	360
B	4	Print	288
	12	Plain	864
C	4	Print	288
D	8	Dark	576
	8	Plain	576

FABRIC REQUIRED

8¾ yards Plain
4½ yards Print
2⅓ yards Dark

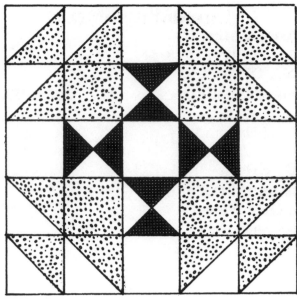

Illus. 170.

This could also be set with alternate plain blocks.

ADD SEAM ALLOWANCES

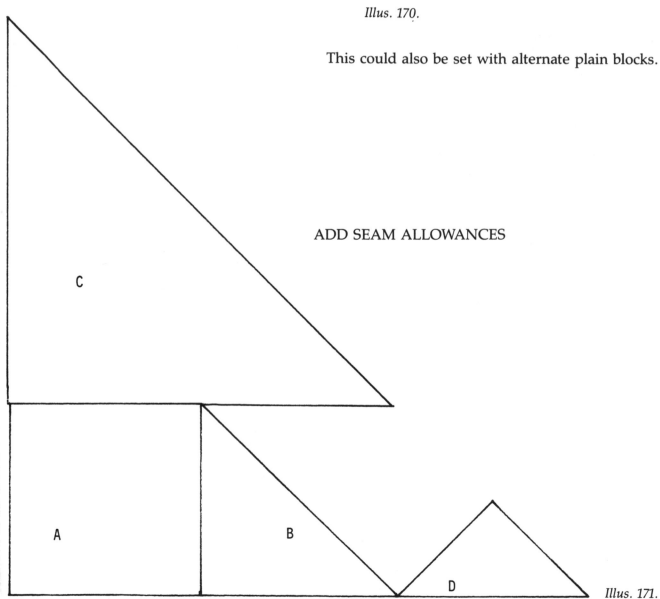

Illus. 171.

Improved 4-Patch

BLOCK SIZE: 8″
QUILT SIZE: 80″ × 80″
NO. OF BLOCKS: 100

This quilt is made entirely from scraps. The scraps can be utilized in several different ways. You can use the diagram to place the various scraps, you can make each piece a different scrap, or you could make the outer triangles all the same color.

The quilt can be set solid, with lattice strips or alternate plain blocks.

Illus. 172.

ADD SEAM ALLOWANCES

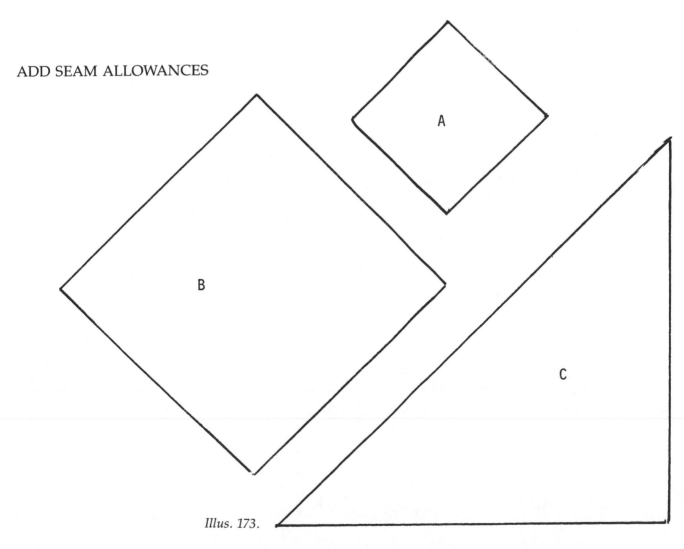

Illus. 173.

115

Indiana Puzzle

BLOCK SIZE: 12"
QUILT SIZE: 84" × 84"
NO. OF BLOCKS: 25 pieced
                 12 Plain
                 12 Print

PIECES PER BLOCK		PER QUILT
A	2 Print	50
	2 Plain	50
B	2 Print	50
	2 Plain	50
C	2 Print	50
	2 Plain	50
D	2 Print	50
	2 Plain	50
E	2 Print	50
	2 Plain	
	12 Plain 13" squares	
	12 Print 13" squares	

FABRIC REQUIRED
5 yards Print
7 yards Plain

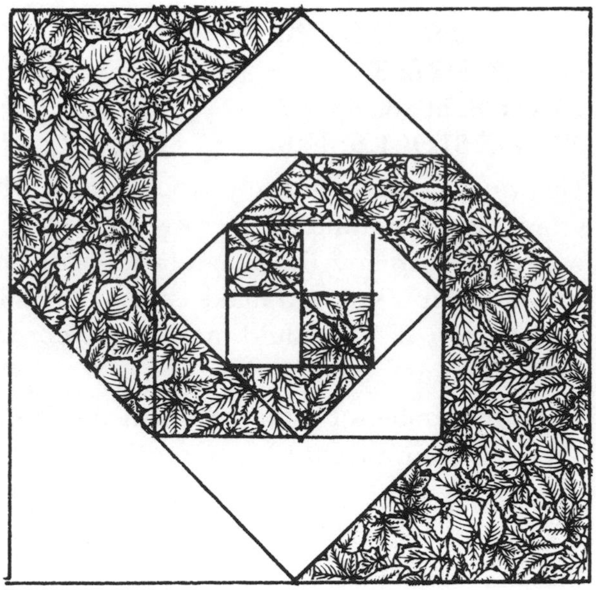

Illus. 174.

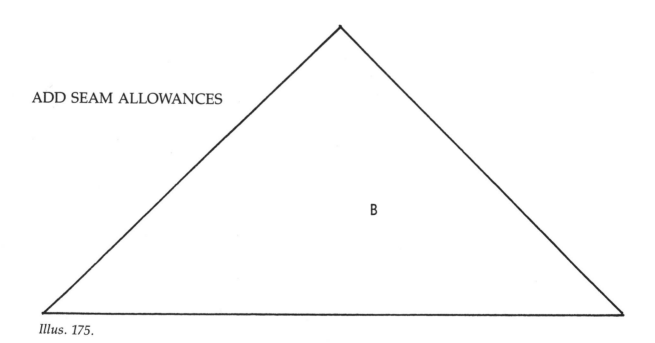

ADD SEAM ALLOWANCES

B

Illus. 175.

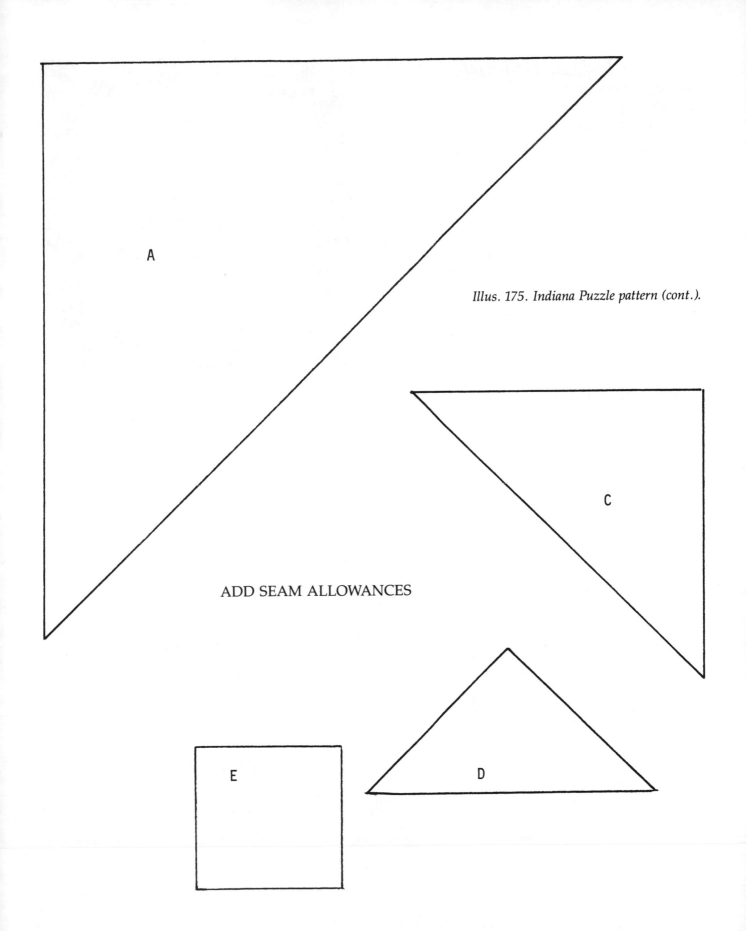

A

Illus. 175. Indiana Puzzle pattern (cont.).

C

ADD SEAM ALLOWANCES

D

E

Indian Hatchet

BLOCK SIZE: 16″
QUILT SIZE: 80″ × 96″
NO. OF BLOCKS: 30

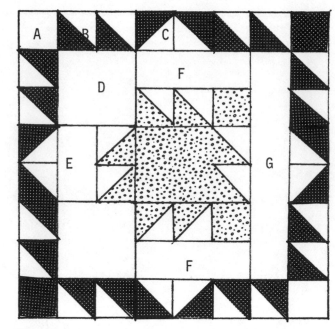

Illus. 176.

PIECES PER BLOCK			PER QUILT
A	2	Dark	60
	2	Print	60
	2	Plain	60
B	24	Dark	720
	8	Print	240
	16	Plain	480
C	4	Plain	120
D	2	Plain	60
	1	Print	30
E	1	Plain	30
F	2	Plain	60
G	1	Plain	30

FABRIC REQUIRED

4¼ yards Dark
2¼ yards Print
8¼ yards Plain

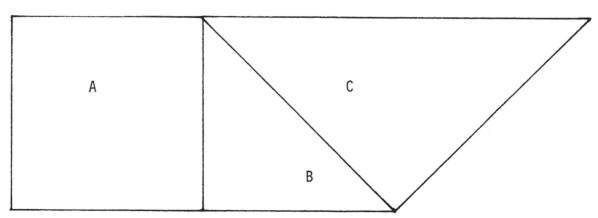

Illus. 177.

ADD SEAM ALLOWANCES

118

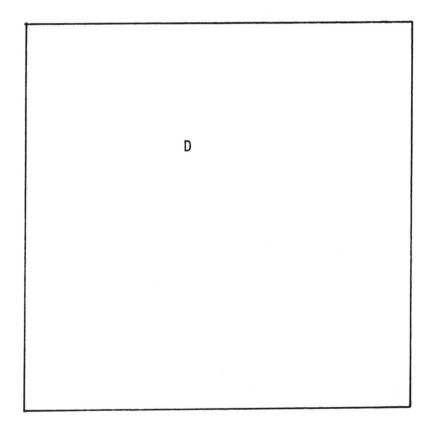

CONTINUE TO SOLID
LINE FOR F

CUT AT DASH LINE FOR E

FOR G, EXTEND TO MEASURE 12"

D

Illus. 177. Indian Hatchet pattern (cont.).

Irish Chain, Double

BLOCK SIZE: 10″
QUILT SIZE: 90″ × 90″
NO. OF BLOCKS: 41A
40B

PIECES PER BLOCK			PER QUILT
BLOCK A:			
C	9	Print	369
	12	Plain	492
	4	White	164
BLOCK B:			
A	1	White	40
B	4	White	160
C	4	Plain	160

FABRIC REQUIRED
2⅛ yards Print
3⅔ yards Plain
4½ yards White

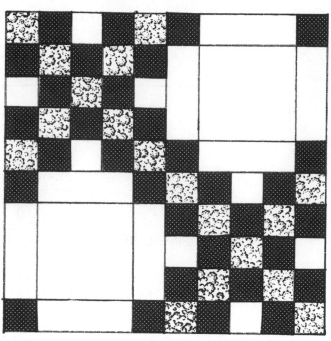

Illus. 178.

Double Irish Chain and Triple Irish Chain use the same pattern pieces with the addition of D to Triple Irish Chain.

Illus. 179.

Irish Chain, Triple

BLOCK SIZE: 14″
QUILT SIZE: 98″ × 98″
NO. OF BLOCKS: 24 A
25 B

PIECES PER BLOCK			PER QUILT
BLOCK A:			
C	4	White	96
	12	Dark	288
	13	Print #1	
	20	Print #2	480
BLOCK B:			
A	1	White	25
C	8	Print #2	200
	8	Dark	200
D	4	White	100

FABRIC REQUIRED
3½ yards White
2¾ yards Dark
1¾ yards Print #1
4 yards Print #2

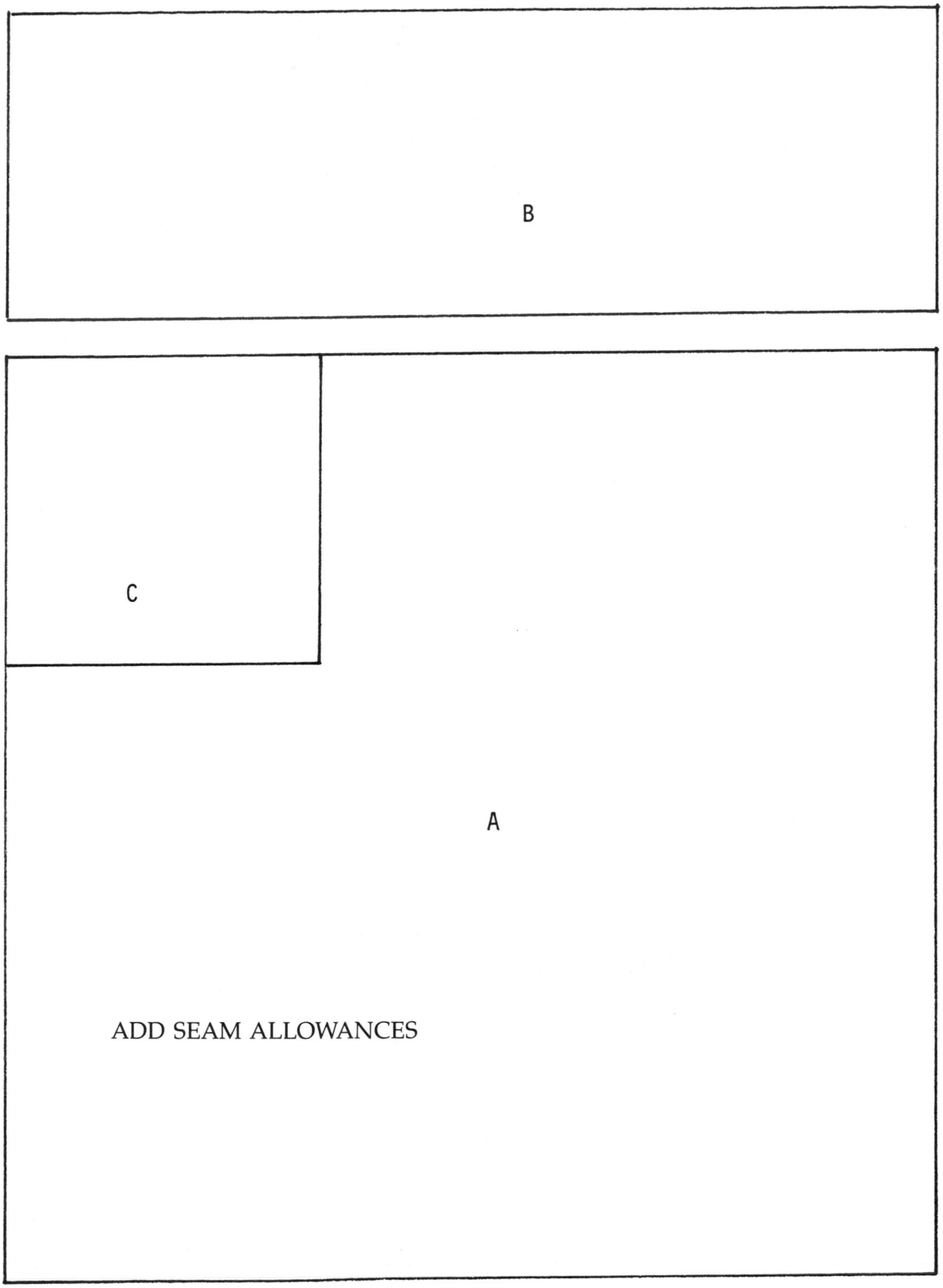

B

C

A

ADD SEAM ALLOWANCES

Illus. 180.

Illus. 181. Triple Irish Chain pattern piece.

Jack-in-the-Box

BLOCK SIZE: 10″
QUILT SIZE: 76″ × 86″
NO. OF BLOCKS: 56
(28 pieced; 28 plain; 7 across by 8 down)

PIECES PER BLOCK		PER QUILT
A	1 White	28
B	4 Red Print	112
C	4 Red	112
D	4 Red	112
E	16 White	448

FABRIC REQUIRED
2½ yards Red
6 yards White
3¼ yards Red Print

BORDER
3″ Red Print strips

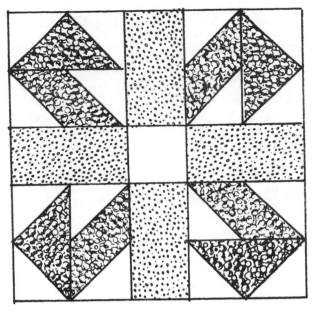

Illus. 182.

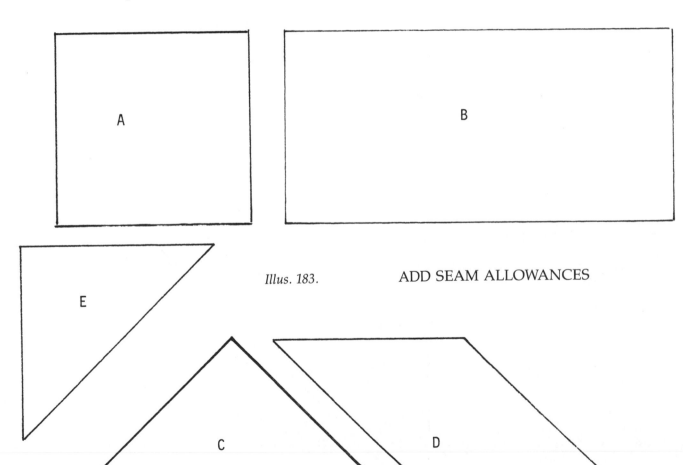

Illus. 183.   ADD SEAM ALLOWANCES

123

Jacob's Ladder

BLOCK SIZE: 12″
QUILT SIZE: 84″ × 96″
NO. OF BLOCKS: 56

PIECES PER BLOCK		PER QUILT
A	10 Dark	560
	10 White	560
B	4 Print	224
	4 White	224

FABRIC REQUIRED
3½ yards Dark
2 yards Print
5½ yards White

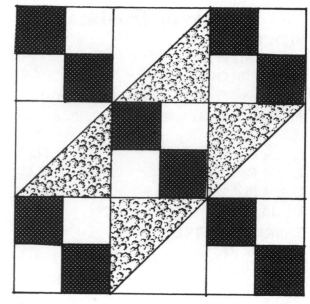

Illus. 184.

ADD SEAM ALLOWANCES

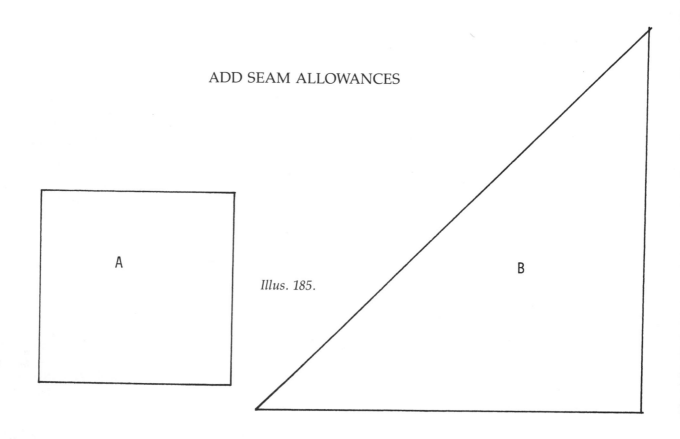

A

Illus. 185.

B

Kansas Troubles

BLOCK SIZE: 12″
QUILT SIZE: 87″ × 99″
NO. OF BLOCKS: 56

PIECES PER BLOCK		PER QUILT
A	4 White	224
	4 Red	224
B	24 White	1344
	24 Red	1344
C	4 White	224

FABRIC REQUIRED
6 yards White
5 yards Red

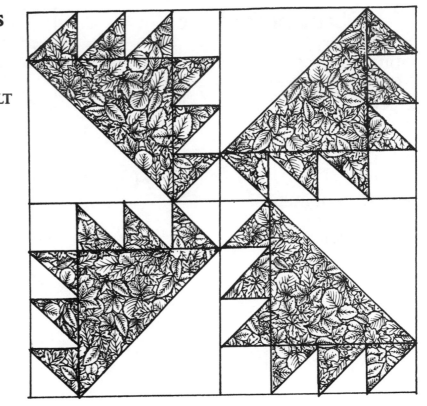

Illus. 186.

ADD SEAM ALLOWANCES

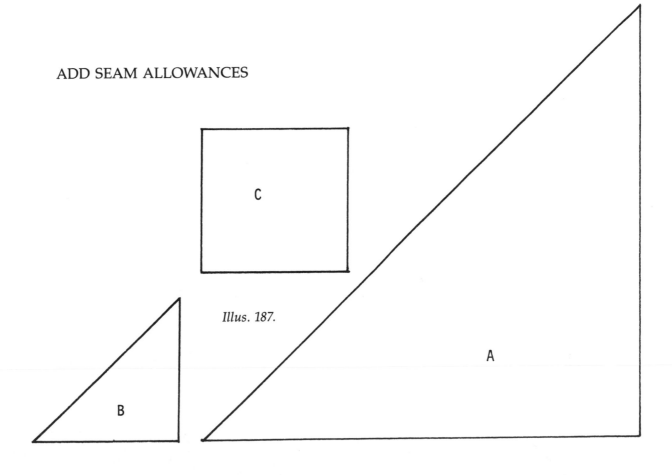

Illus. 187.

125

Lady of the Lake

BLOCK SIZE: 10″
QUILT SIZE: 80″ × 80″
NO. OF BLOCKS: 64

PIECES PER BLOCK		PER QUILT
A	16 Print	1024
	16 Plain	1024
B	1 Print	64
	1 Plain	64

FABRIC REQUIRED
6¾ yards Print
6¾ yards Plain

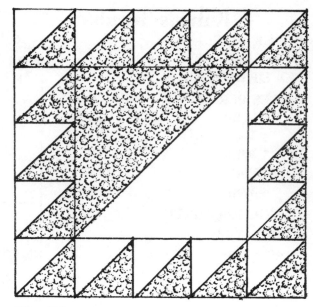

Illus. 188.

ADD SEAM ALLOWANCES

Illus. 189.

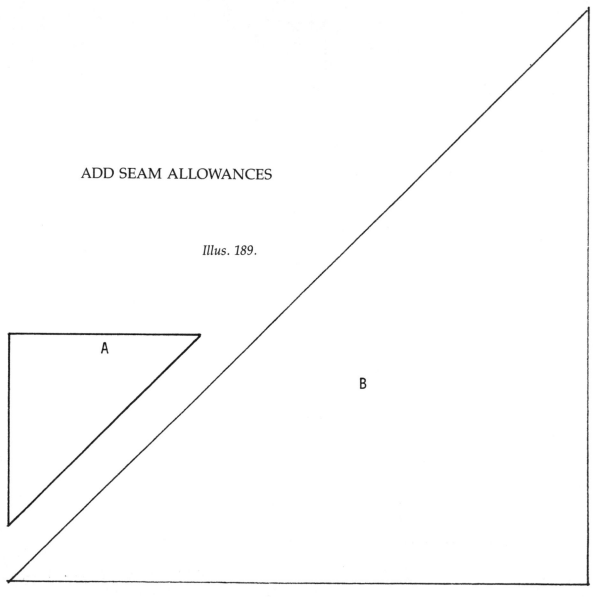

A

B

Milky Way

BLOCK SIZE: 12"
QUILT SIZE: 84" × 84"

PIECES PER QUILT

A	Dark	242
	White	242
B	Print	220
	White	220
C	Print	50
	White	50

Illus. 190.

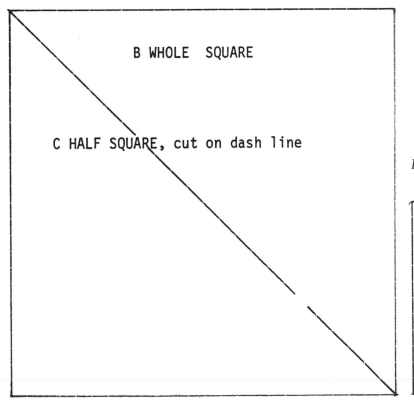

B WHOLE SQUARE

C HALF SQUARE, cut on dash line

ADD SEAM ALLOWANCES

Illus. 191.

A

Ohio Star

BLOCK SIZE: 12"
QUILT SIZE: 84" × 84"
NO. OF BLOCKS: 49

PIECES PER BLOCK		PER QUILT
A	8 White	392
	8 Print	392
B	4 White	196
	1 Print	49

FABRIC REQUIRED

This is usually made as a scrap quilt with a different print for each block. If you prefer to use the same print throughout, you will need:
4 yards Print
6½ yards White

Illus. 192.

ADD SEAM ALLOWANCES

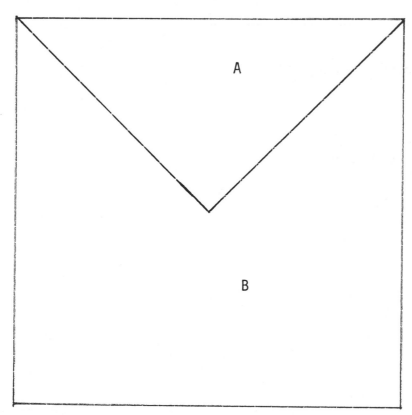

Illus. 193.

Pine Tree

BLOCK SIZE: 20″
QUILT SIZE: 85″ × 85″
NO. OF BLOCKS: 9

PIECES PER BLOCK			PER QUILT
A	3	White	27
B	42	Green Print	378
	36	White	324
C	3	White	27
D	2	Dark Green	18
E	2	Dark Green	18
F	2	White	18
G	1	Dark Green	9

Blocks are set on the diagonal
    4 White 21″ squares
    8 White Half-squares
    4 White Quarter-squares

FABRIC REQUIRED
6⅔ yards White
2 yards Green Print
1¼ yards Dark Green or Brown

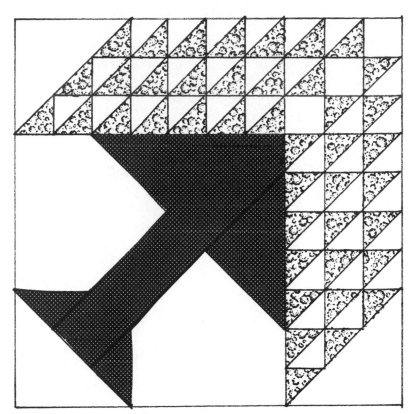

Illus. 194.

ADD SEAM ALLOWANCES

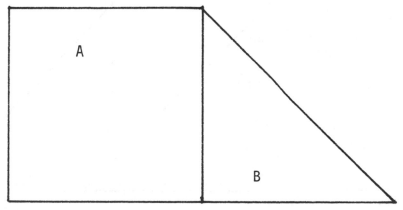

Illus. 195.

129

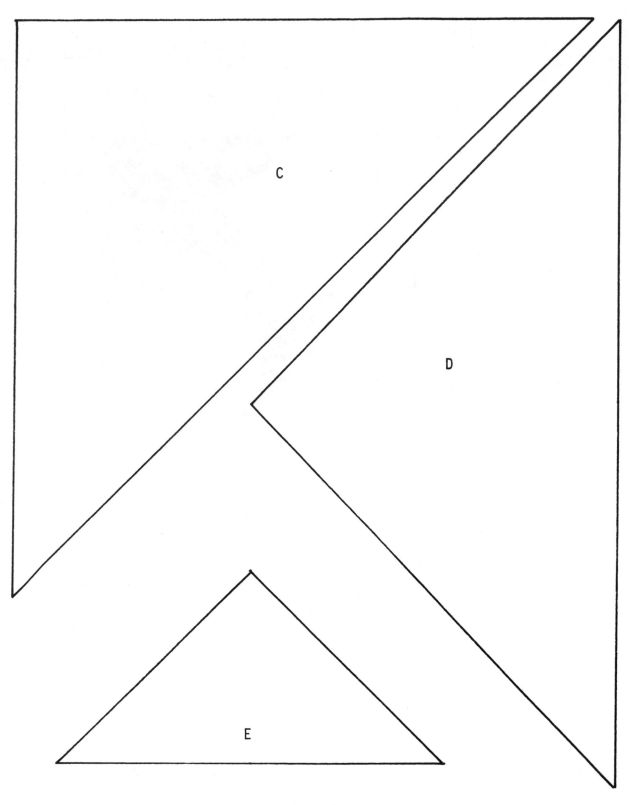

ADD SEAM ALLOWANCES

Illus. 195. Pine Tree pattern (cont.).

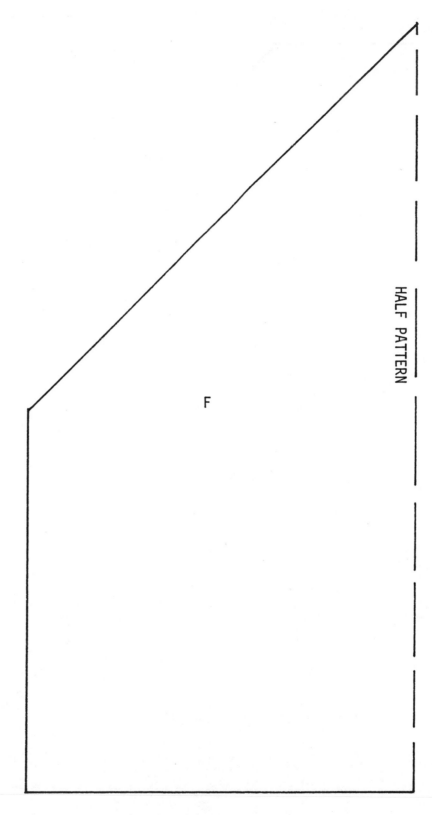

HALF PATTERN

F

ADD SEAM ALLOWANCES

Illus. 195. Pine Tree pattern (cont.).

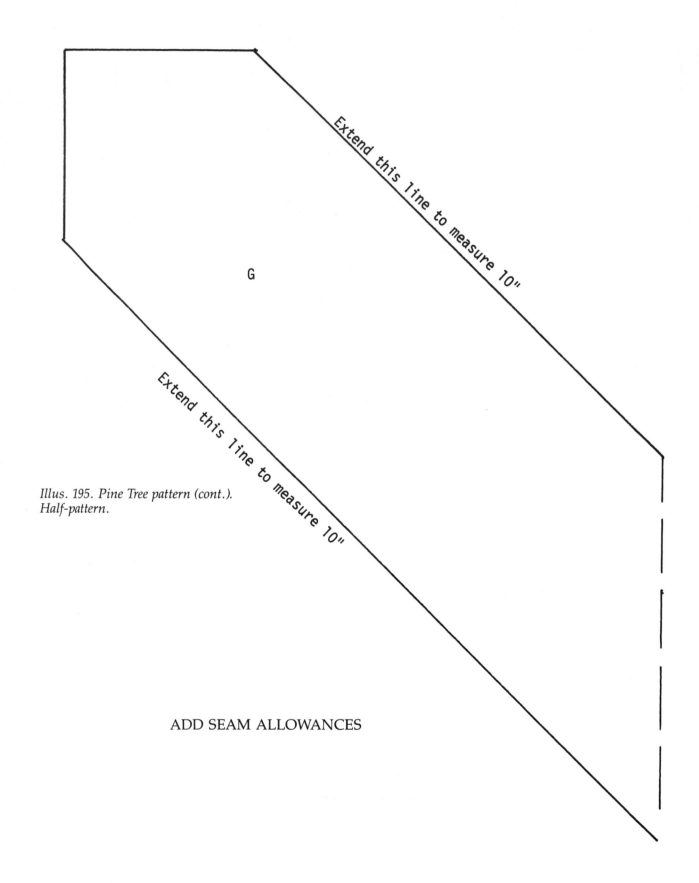

Extend this line to measure 10"

Extend this line to measure 10"

G

Illus. 195. Pine Tree pattern (cont.).
Half-pattern.

ADD SEAM ALLOWANCES

Pinwheel Square Variation

BLOCK SIZE: 15″
QUILT SIZE: 75″ × 90″
NO. OF BLOCKS: 30

PIECES PER BLOCK			PER QUILT
A	5	Print	150
B	4	Plain	120
C	4	Print	120
D	4	Print	120
	4	Plain	120
E	4	Plain	120

FABRIC REQUIRED
4¾ yards Print
5 yards Plain

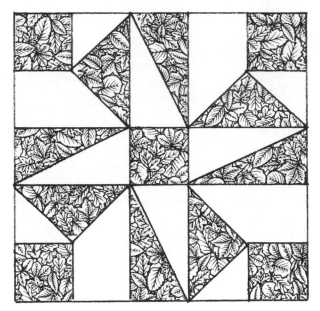

Illus. 196.

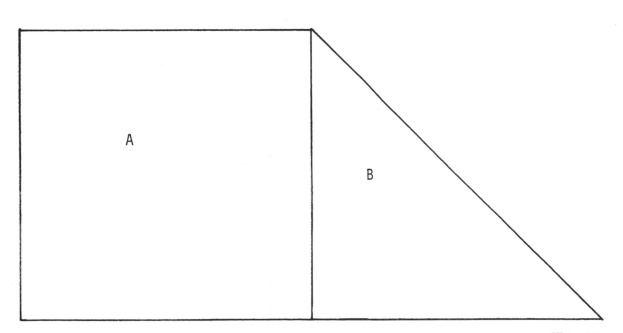

Illus. 197.

ADD SEAM ALLOWANCES

133

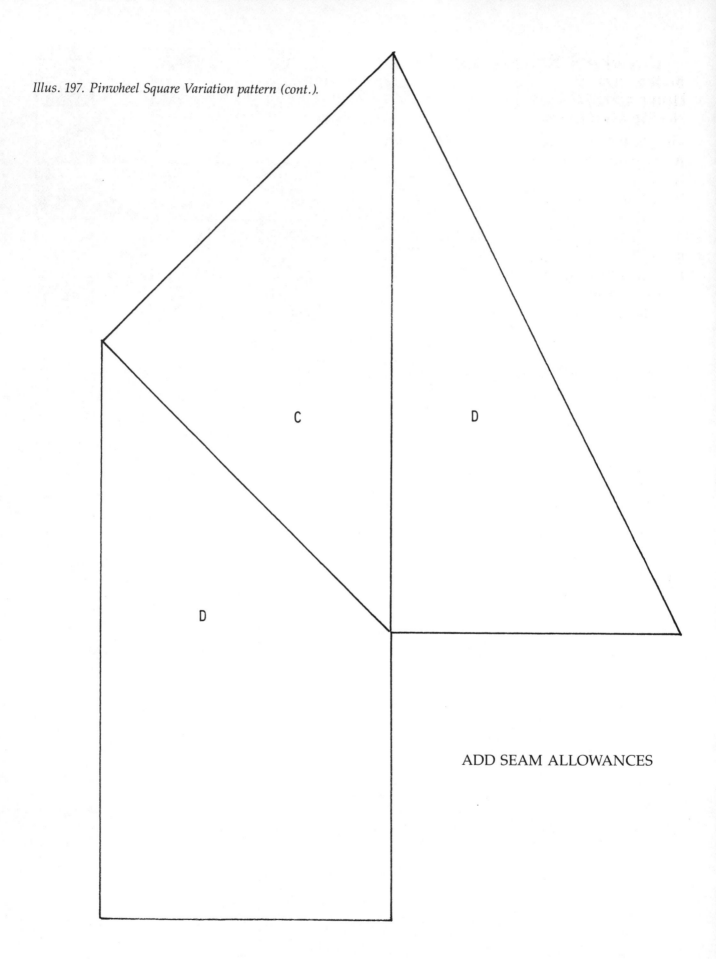

Illus. 197. Pinwheel Square Variation pattern (cont.).

C

D

D

ADD SEAM ALLOWANCES

Shoofly

BLOCK SIZE: 6″
QUILT SIZE: 72″ × 84″
NO. OF BLOCKS: 168

This is an all scrap quilt

PIECES PER BLOCK
A   4 Print
B   1 Plain

FABRIC REQUIRED
Per block, A requires a 9½″ × 4½″ piece
B requires a 5½″ square

Illus. 198.

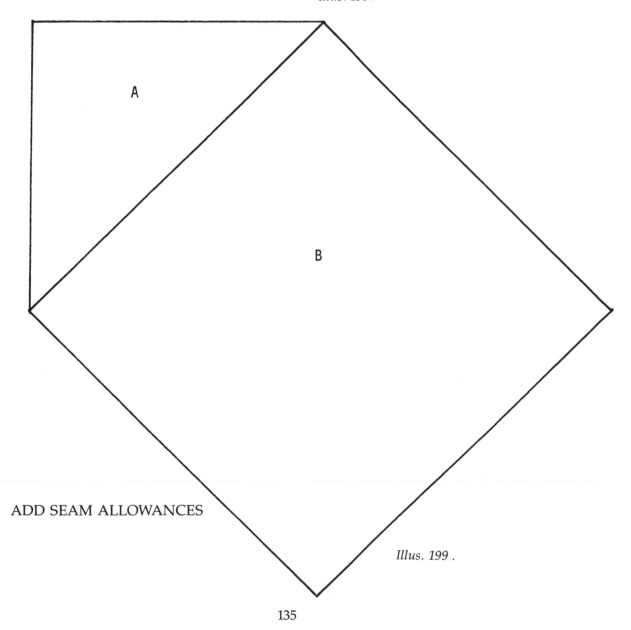

ADD SEAM ALLOWANCES

Illus. 199.

Strawberry Basket

BLOCK SIZE: 12″
QUILT SIZE: 85″ × 85″
NO. OF BLOCKS: 25 Pieced
25 Plain

Diagonal Set

PIECES PER BLOCK		PER QUILT
A	6 Dark	150
	9 White	225
B	6 Dark	150
C	2 Dark	50
	1 Dark Print	25
D	2 Light Print	50

FABRIC REQUIRED

5 yards White
2 yards Dark
1½ yards Light Print
½ yard Dark Print

Illus. 200.

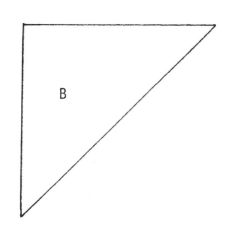

A

ADD SEAM ALLOWANCES

B

Illus. 201.

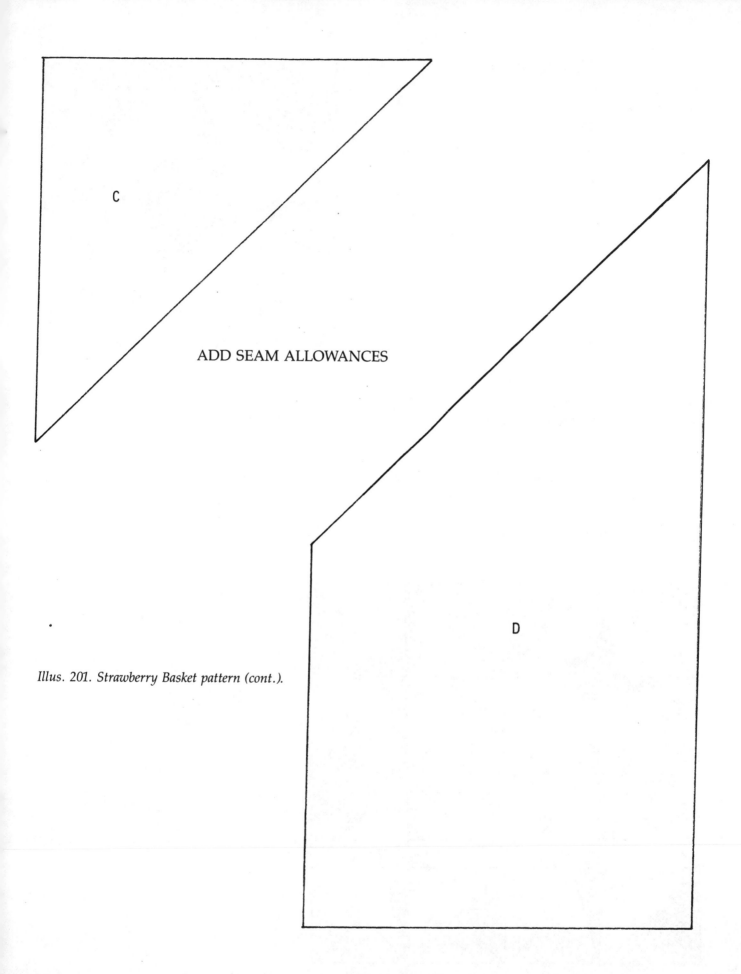

C

ADD SEAM ALLOWANCES

D

Illus. 201. Strawberry Basket pattern (cont.).

Waste Not

BLOCK SIZE: 12″
QUILT SIZE: 84″ × 84″
NO. OF BLOCKS: 49

PIECES PER BLOCK	PER QUILT
A 4 Print	196
B 4 Assorted Prints	196
C 4 White	196

FABRIC REQUIRED
4⅛ yards Print
4½ yards White

Illus. 202.

B is a scrap piece changing from block to block. A could also be treated as a scrap, if desired, changing from block to block, or you could use four prints within each block.

The diagram below shows a slight variation of this design which allows you to use even more scraps. Part A is cut as shown by the dash line on the pattern piece. When the prints are arranged as shown below, a secondary pinwheel pattern emerges. Scraps could also be used randomly.

Illus. 203.

138

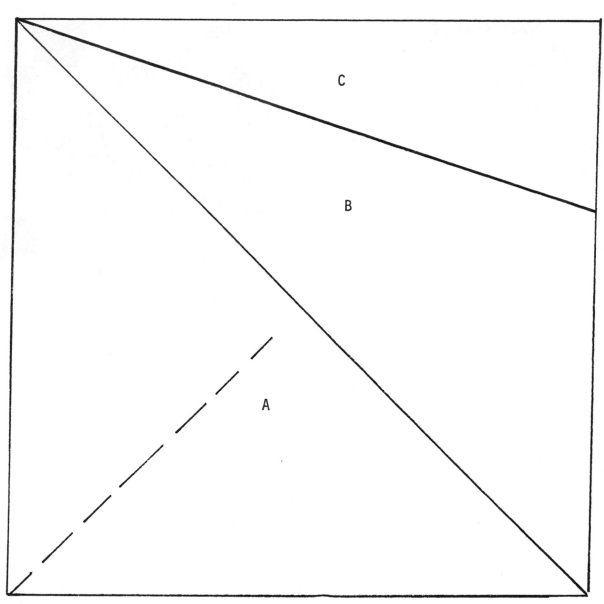

Illus. 204.

ADD SEAM ALLOWANCES

Waterwheel

BLOCK SIZE: 12″
QUILT SIZE: 84″ × 84″
NO. OF BLOCKS: 49

PIECES PER BLOCK		PER QUILT
A	4 Dark	196
	8 White	392
	4 Light Print	196
	2 Dark Print	98
B	2 Light Print	98
	2 Dark Print	98
	4 White	196

FABRIC REQUIRED
4 yards White
1 yard Dark
2 yards Light Print
1¾ yards Dark Print

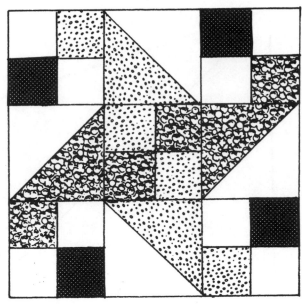

Illus. 205.

ADD SEAM ALLOWANCES

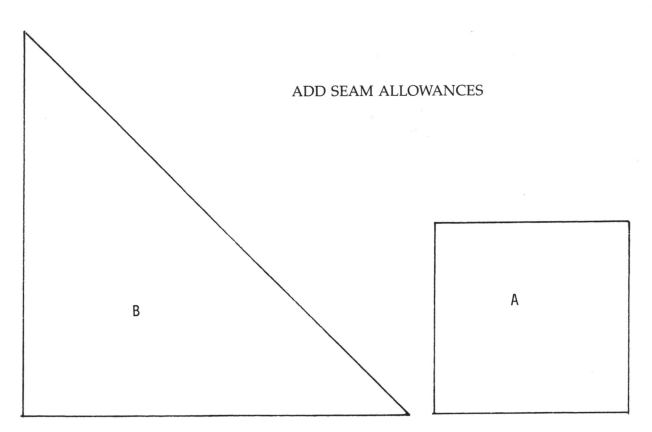

B

A

Illus. 206.

World Without End

BLOCK SIZE: 16″
QUILT SIZE: 80″ × 96″
NO. OF BLOCKS: 30

PIECES PER BLOCK		PER QUILT
A	8 Print	240
	8 Plain	240
B	8 Print	240
	8 Plain	240
C	2 Print	60
	2 Plain	60

FABRIC REQUIRED

5½ yards Print
5½ yards Plain

Illus. 207.

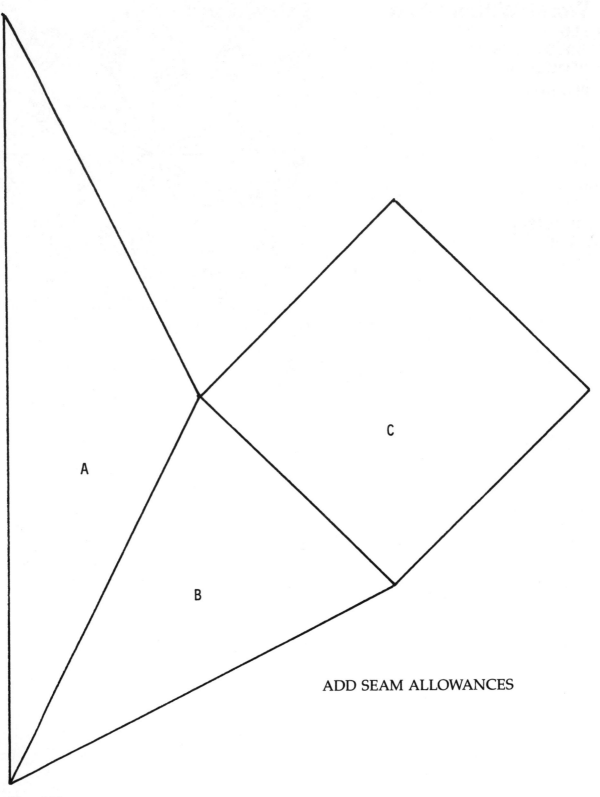

A

B

C

ADD SEAM ALLOWANCES

Illus. 208.

SHORTCUT QUILTING PATTERNS

All of the quilting patterns which follow can be machine-stitched and are adaptable to the shortcut methods shown in the chapter on Quilting.

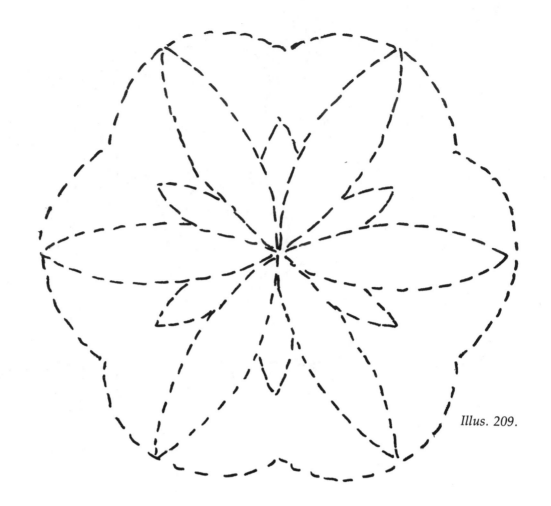

Illus. 209.

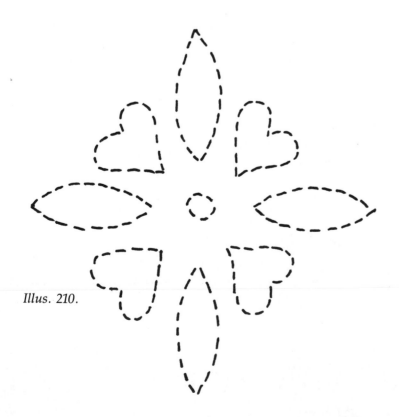

Illus. 210.

145

Illus. 211.

Illus. 212.

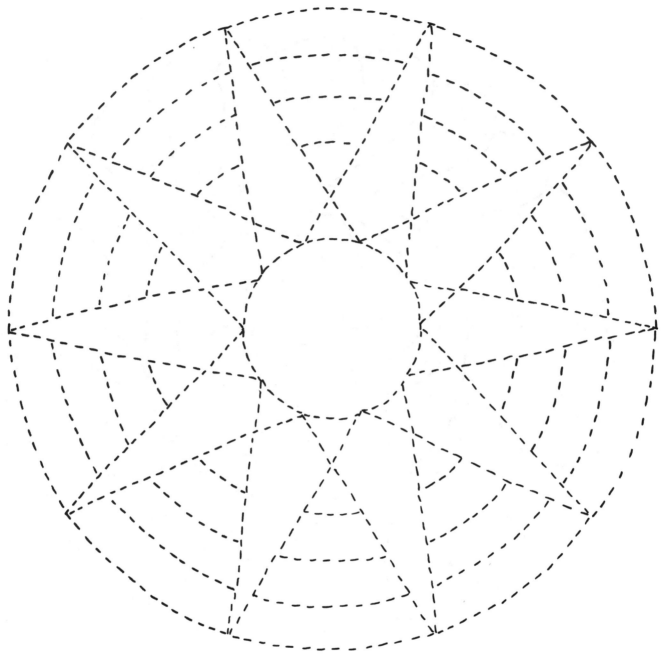

Illus. 213.

Illus. 214.

Illus. 215.

149

Illus. 216.

Illus. 217.

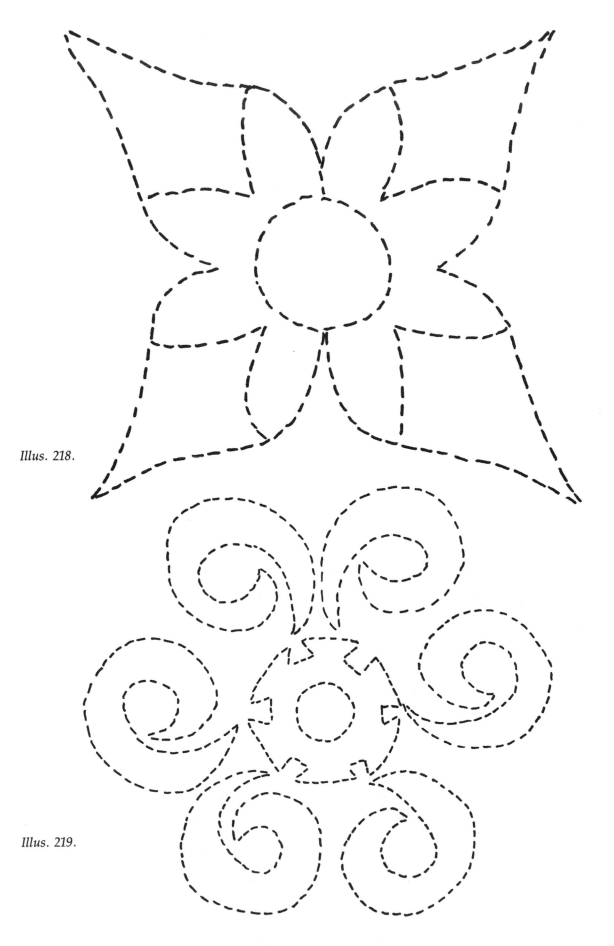

Illus. 218.

Illus. 219.

151

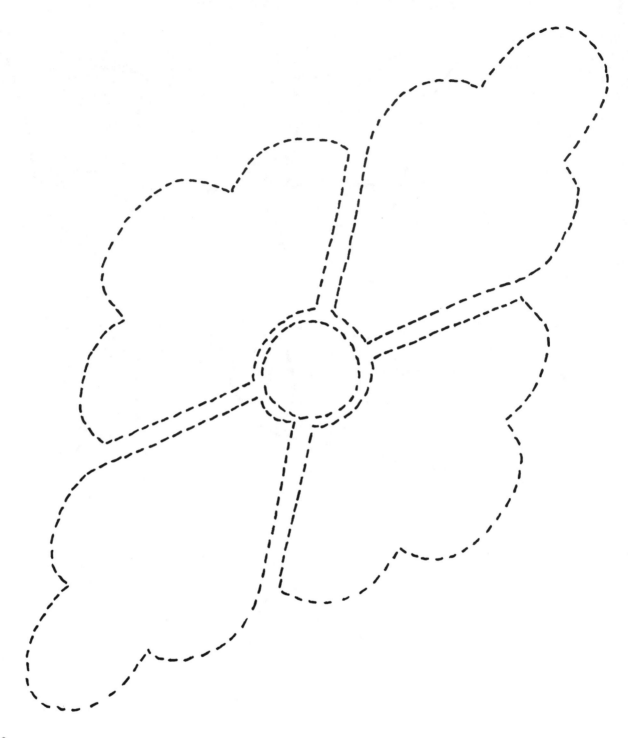

Illus. 220.

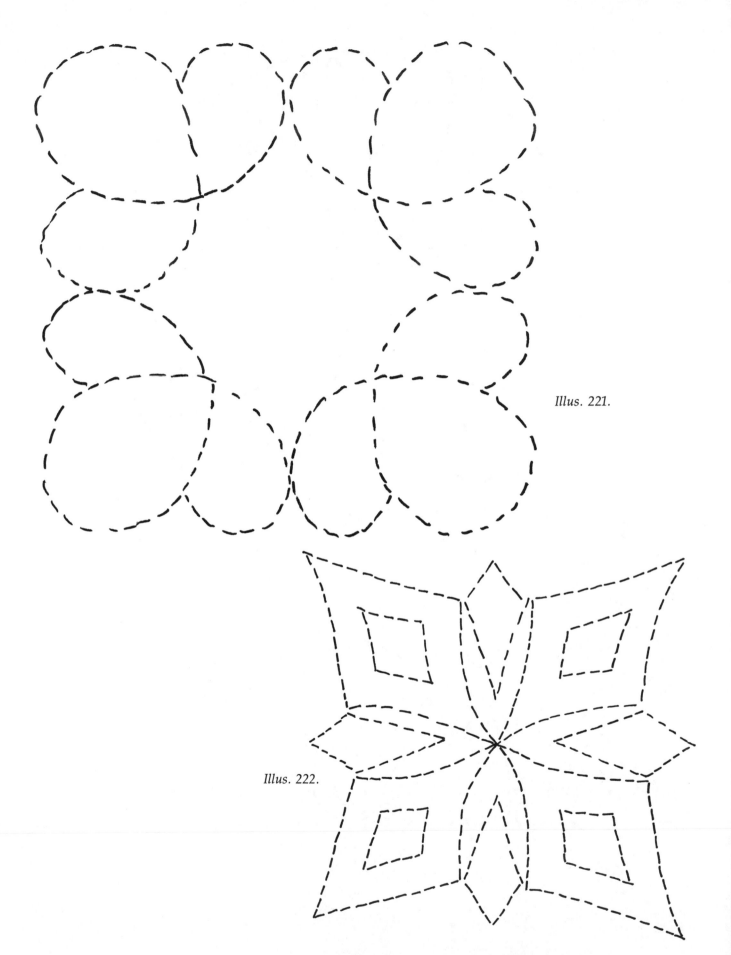

Illus. 221.

Illus. 222.

153

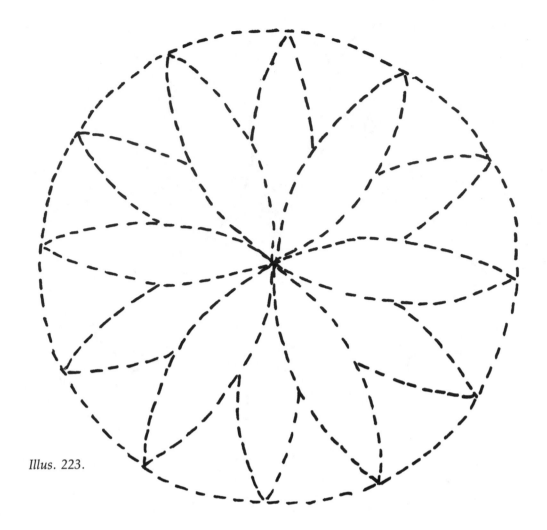

Illus. 223.

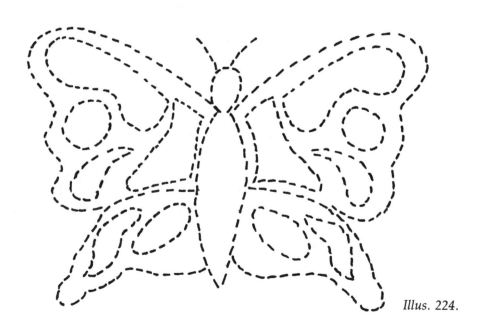

Illus. 224.

154

Illus. 225.

155

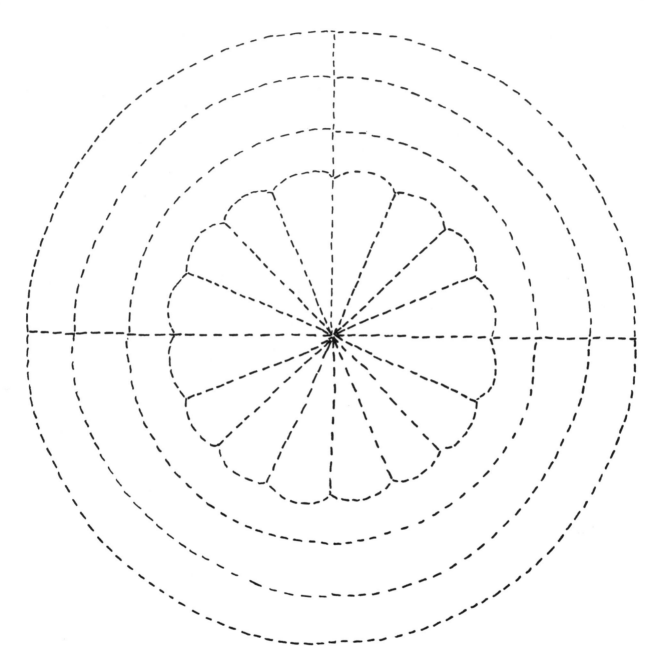

Illus. 226. The three lines going out to the edge illustrate the various ways in which this design can be used.

Illus. 227.

Illus. 228.　　　　*Illus. 229.*　　　　*Illus. 230.*

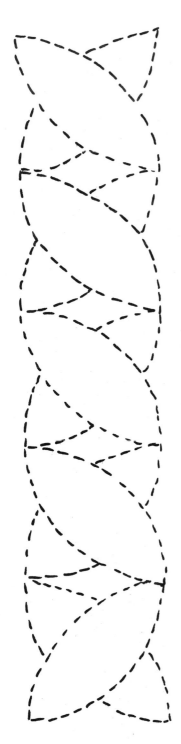

Illus. 231.

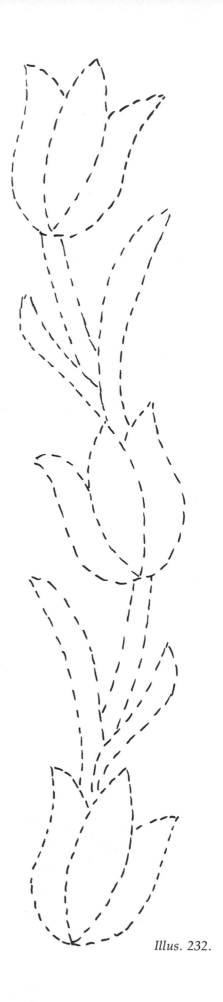

Illus. 232.

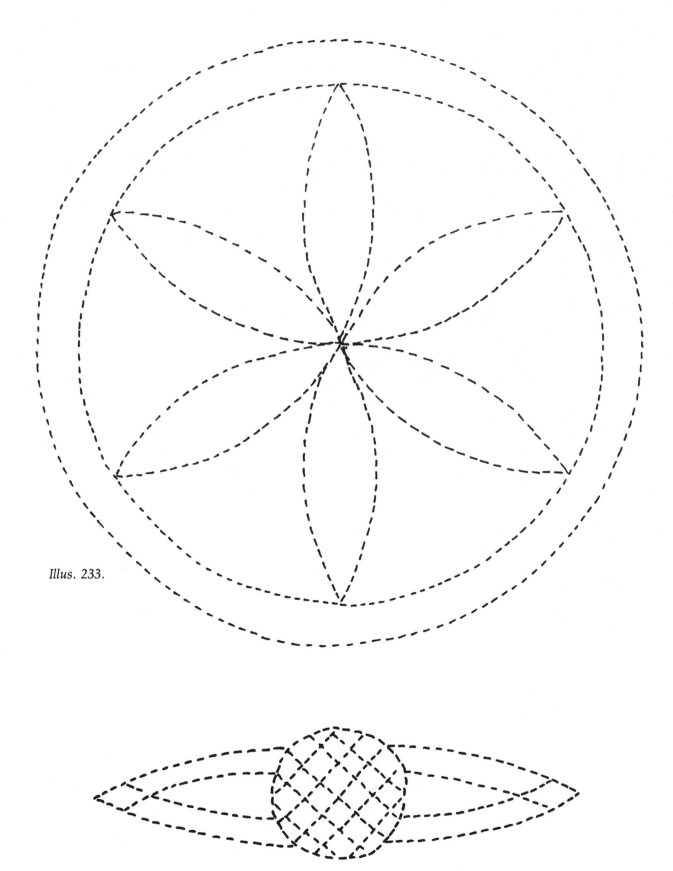

Illus. 233.

Illus. 234.

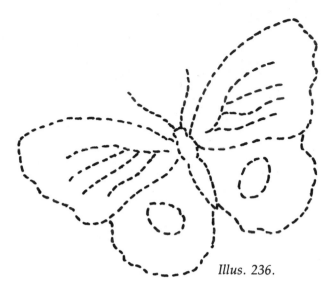

Illus. 236.

Illus. 235.

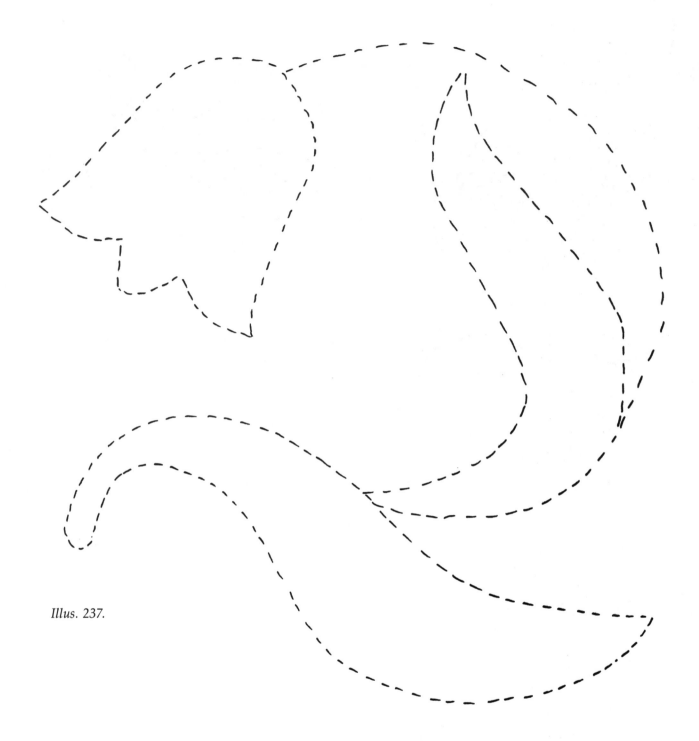

Illus. 237.

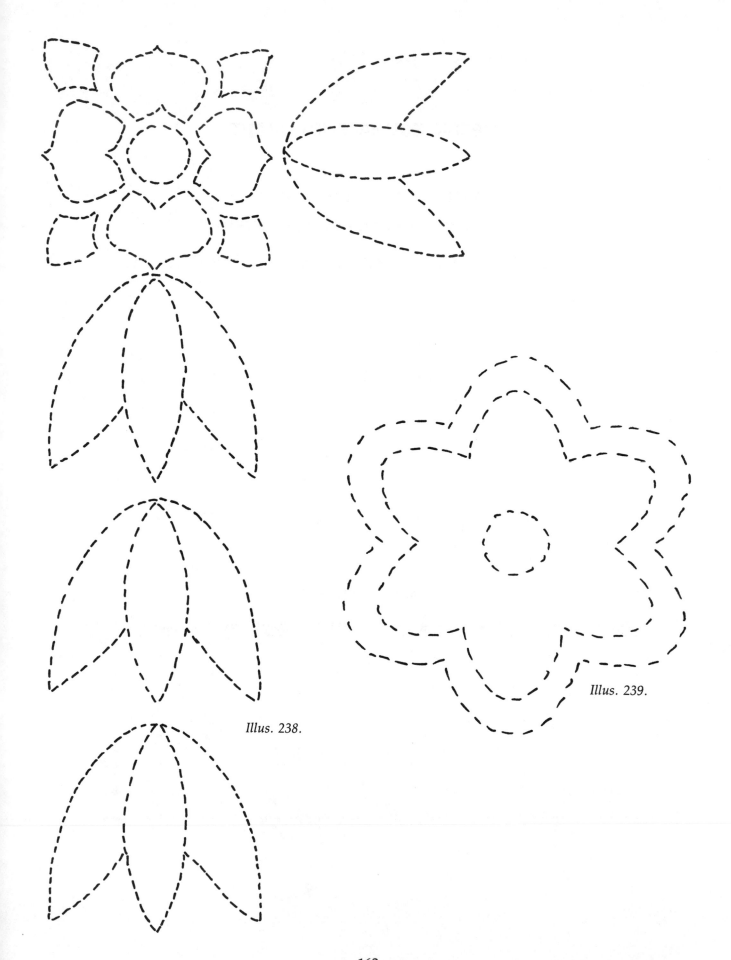

Illus. 238.

Illus. 239.

163

METRIC EQUIVALENCY CHART

MM—MILLIMETRES   CM—CENTIMETRES

INCHES TO MILLIMETRES AND CENTIMETRES

INCHES	MM	CM	INCHES	CM	INCHES	CM
⅛	3	0.3	9	22.9	30	76.2
¼	6	0.6	10	25.4	31	78.7
⅜	10	1.0	11	27.9	32	81.3
½	13	1.3	12	30.5	33	83.8
⅝	16	1.6	13	33.0	34	86.4
¾	19	1.9	14	35.6	35	88.9
⅞	22	2.2	15	38.1	36	91.4
1	25	2.5	16	40.6	37	94.0
1¼	32	3.2	17	43.2	38	96.5
1½	38	3.8	18	45.7	39	99.1
1¾	44	4.4	19	48.3	40	101.6
2	51	5.1	20	50.8	41	104.1
2½	64	6.4	21	53.3	42	106.7
3	76	7.6	22	55.9	43	109.2
3½	89	8.9	23	58.4	44	111.8
4	102	10.2	24	61.0	45	114.3
4½	114	11.4	25	63.5	46	116.8
5	127	12.7	26	66.0	47	119.4
6	152	15.2	27	68.6	48	121.9
7	178	17.8	28	71.1	49	124.5
8	203	20.3	29	73.7	50	127.0

YARDS TO METRES

YARDS	METRES	YARDS	METRES	YARDS	METRES	YARDS	METRES	YARDS	METRES
⅛	0.11	2⅛	1.94	4⅛	3.77	6⅛	5.60	8⅛	7.43
¼	0.23	2¼	2.06	4¼	3.89	6¼	5.72	8¼	7.54
⅜	0.34	2⅜	2.17	4⅜	4.00	6⅜	5.83	8⅜	7.66
½	0.46	2½	2.29	4½	4.11	6½	5.94	8½	7.77
⅝	0.57	2⅝	2.40	4⅝	4.23	6⅝	6.06	8⅝	7.89
¾	0.69	2¾	2.51	4¾	4.34	6¾	6.17	8¾	8.00
⅞	0.80	2⅞	2.63	4⅞	4.46	6⅞	6.29	8⅞	8.12
1	0.91	3	2.74	5	4.57	7	6.40	9	8.23
1⅛	1.03	3⅛	2.86	5⅛	4.69	7⅛	6.52	9⅛	8.34
1¼	1.14	3¼	2.97	5¼	4.80	7¼	6.63	9¼	8.46
1⅜	1.26	3⅜	3.09	5⅜	4.91	7⅜	6.74	9⅜	8.57
1½	1.37	3½	3.20	5½	5.03	7½	6.86	9½	8.69
1⅝	1.49	3⅝	3.31	5⅝	5.14	7⅝	6.97	9⅝	8.80
1¾	1.60	3¾	3.43	5¾	5.26	7¾	7.09	9¾	8.92
1⅞	1.71	3⅞	3.54	5⅞	5.37	7⅞	7.20	9⅞	9.03
2	1.83	4	3.66	6	5.49	8	7.32	10	9.14

INDEX